TI..
REAL
ALE
CANARY

THE REAL ALE CANARY

A SPLENDID RUSH THROUGH A FINE CITY DURING THE 2021–2022 FOOTBALL SEASON

bannister publications

NEIL COLLINGS

First published in Great Britain in 2022 by
Bannister Publications Ltd
118 Saltergate, Chesterfield, Derbyshire S40 1NG

Copyright © Neil Collings 2022

ISBN: 978-1-909813-88-5

Typeset by Bannister Publications Ltd
Cover illustration by Imogen Worthington

Printed and bound by CMP UK Ltd, in Great Britain

This book was self-published by Bannister Publications.
For more information on self-publishing visit:
www.bannisterpublications.com

NORWICH CITY

– a poem by Harry Exford (June 2021)

Concentration gone as hard as I try
The Canaries at home the reason why
Manchester United the team to beat
Stars aplenty – magical feet

We've reached the top without a doubt
Time for supporters to jump and shout
Norwich City are here to stay
Everyone's yelling "Hip Hip Hooray"

We're dressed tip to toe in Yellow and Green
So much colour you've never seen
Wherever you turn it's always there
Other colours – you wouldn't dare!

You can feel the excitement before every match
The build up tremendous as a sandwich they snatch
In the ground expectations high
We've beaten the best – hung them out to dry

We're afraid of no one including Man U
We've beaten the best only lost to a few
Norwich City are bound for the top
Onwards and upwards – we'll never stop!

CONTENTS

INTRODUCTION

It's not as though I amble around the city of Norwich sporting a tweed flat cap, my small, sleek whippet on a long, unthreatening leash while scoffing a black pudding and dripping butty - that's me, not the dog. It's not as though I acknowledge all the native blokes with an "ow a'tha me owd cocker" or all the resident ladies with an "orate duck".

But nevertheless, the locals are onto me. They know.

"You're no' from round 'are aare yow bor" (you are not from around here are you my good man) is a rhetorical question I am often asked. More frequently and pertinently though, I am probed with the million-dollar question "hew cum yow suppor' Norridge?" and being born and bred in Chesterfield, Derbyshire, this is a valid query.

I will now attempt to answer the second question, but this will have to be in a roundabout way – in fact, there will probably be more roundabouts than there are on the A17 and A47 combined.

My parents/grandparents owned a caravan in Mablethorpe and I used to spend a great deal of my school holidays in the Lincolnshire seaside town in the early 1970s. As a football-mad youngster, still not in my teens, I used to eagerly await the Sunday afternoon highlights package 'Match of the Week' on Anglia TV hosted by Gerry Harrison. I had little interest in most of the other sides which sometimes featured, such as Luton Town, Cambridge United or, god forbid, Ipswich, but somewhere along the way I developed a penchant for Norwich City. This feeling was only enhanced during one of the games when my grandmother Evelyn, who had hardly ever shown any interest in the programme, enquired, "Is this Norwich who's playing?" After an affirmative nod, she then regaled me with a most wonderful story about the football club and its supporters – I told you there would be roundabouts.

She told me about a special day on 28th February 1959 when the supporters of Third Division Norwich City were on their way to play Division Two Sheffield United (nicknamed The Blades) in an epic FA Cup 6th Round Tie. Evelyn owned a small grocers shop in the North East Derbyshire mining village of Clowne, which just happened to be on the direct route the City supporters were travelling on to the hosts' Bramall Lane ground.

She told me of the seemingly never-ending yellow and green cavalcade making its way to the Steel City that day as literally thousands of "happy, smiling, wonderful" people made their way, many of them stopping off at her shop for pop and snacks.

Apparently, the good people of Clowne were so taken and impressed with the Norfolk temporary migration that after the game (that ended in a 1-1 draw) they went out onto the streets and applauded them on their return journey. "I've always had a soft spot for Norwich ever since" Evelyn added.

A few days later, on Wednesday 4th March 1959, Norwich was to win the replay 3-2 in a five-goal thriller in a truly pulsating clash that put them through to their first ever FA Cup Semi-Final (that they subsequently lost, again after a replay). Arguably, it was this cup run from the first round all the way to the last four that really put Norwich City on the footballing map.

Evelyn's soft spot must have been contagious as I was now on a mission to see The Canaries in the flesh. The next (and penultimate) roundabout, therefore, lay extremely close-by to my Chesterfield home as it took me onto the 12 mile stretch to the scene of the 1-1 draw mentioned above. This time, it was the turn of my other grandparent (and Evelyn's husband), Fred, to step into the spotlight. It was January 1973, and I had been eyeing the fixture list with a sense of excitement for a while with City due to play The Blades on the 27th of the month. Fred, even though he was no stranger to football stadiums, nevertheless took some serious persuasion before agreeing to take me to the game.

I must confess that I remember very little about this game other than acknowledging that Norwich hadn't played particularly well in a 2-0 defeat. What I do remember, on returning to my grandparent's home afterwards, is listening to Evelyn asking Fred how the afternoon had been? He told her that he thought I'd enjoyed it but that "I don't think he'll want to watch Norwich again as they're blumming rubbish!" To my grandfather's complete surprise, the opposite happened though, as I was now hooked.

While writing this introduction over 48 years after the event, I was intrigued to find out if something, anything had occurred during the game that had triggered me to become even more dedicated to the Canary cause. I then had the good fortune to actually track down one of The Blades' scorers that afternoon, Billy Dearden.

"Why do you want to know about that game?" inquired Billy, now in his late seventies, after I had telephoned him one Sunday morning. I proudly informed him that I was a Norwich City season ticket holder – "Bad luck with that!" – and that it had been the first where I had seen them live. "No, can't remember that game at all."

So, there we have it. I have something in common with Billy Dearden (and no, it's not that I also scored 24 goals one season in the First Division!). We both remember next to nothing from this fixture.

It was to be another three years before I made my spectator debut at Carrow Road, again the opposition was Sheffield United. The roundabout on this occasion was to take me onto the A17, a road that is now so familiar. All the stars had aligned for me to be able to go to the game. My cousin, Ian, worked for the Sheffield Star/Green 'Un (the equivalent to Norwich Evening News/Pink Un) and was the chief reporter for all Sheffield Wednesday games. The stroke of luck occurred when the Editor asked him to cover the Blades' game at Norwich as he wanted the Sheffield United reporter, Tony Pritchett, to cover that day's FA Cup semi-final between Derby and Manchester United that was to be played at Hillsborough.

I had a truly wonderful day with a bonus trip to Great Yarmouth thrown in, where my cousin interviewed the Sheffield United players pre-match, plus a complimentary seat in the Main Stand and finished off with a walk along the bank of the River Wensum. Indeed a truly cracking day, other than the result, as the already-relegated Sheffield United duly upset the form book and won 3-1. Again then, nothing magical happened on the football front in my first home game, no singular spectacular incident that cemented me as a Norwich City supporter.

So, in conclusion to the 'million dollar question', I can honestly and truthfully answer "Oi ain' go' a clue bor!" No family match day devotion enticing me, no remarkable games or goals at the outset to seduce me, just a strange, almost peculiar sort of belonging.

Now, onto my account of my travels to, from and within the Fine City of Norwich during the 2021-2022 Premier League season, underpinned by Norwich City's 19 home league games.

Oh, I'll also be taking you into a few pubs along the journey...

CHAPTER 1
LIVERPOOL (H)
14TH AUGUST 2021

After the record-breaking, Championship winning 2020-2021 season for Norwich City Football Club, here we are then, back in the Premier League promised land, flowing with milk and honey.

More importantly though, here we are, back at a full-house Carrow Road, choruses of 'On The Ball City' and an overall match day experience that we have missed out on for 18 months since the Leicester City game on the 28th February 2020 due to the coronavirus pandemic.

Here we also are, back at the home of nuclear-temperature pies and fans in replica shirts that stimulate pungent body odours similar to the combined aromas of stilton and fermented fish. How I've missed it (or should that be how have I missed it?)

And here we also are, back at the mercies of a football club ticket office with whom I have had a few 'discussions' recently. Back in July 2020, I had purchased a season ticket in the Main Stand, a change of area for me after over 10 years in the Upper Barclay. I had stressed that I required an aisle seat and was confidently assured by the member of staff that this was exactly what I'd spent my hard-earned £500 on. I was vaguely familiar with the layout and seat numbers in my new 'home', having made a couple of guest appearances there the previous season. However, this seat didn't feel as if it was anywhere other than in the middle of a row. Still, I had to believe what I was being advised, didn't I? After all, surely they had the stadium seating plan in front of them whilst selling me the ticket.

My pre-match had started much earlier in the day at the awesome Fat Cat on West End Street (just off Dereham Road), accompanied by my wife, the delectable Denise. I love their beers; she loves their ciders = a win-win situation. An early optimistic prediction amongst the locals was that today's opposition, Liverpool, would be a formidable challenge, as always, but that City may just catch them on an off day with it being the beginning of the season and all that.

It was an uncomfortable fact that Norwich had experienced a somewhat disjointed and arguably chaotic pre-season with an influx of new signings, plus an exodus of players who were mainly out of contract or considered surplus to requirements by Sporting Director, Stuart Webber and Head Coach, Daniel Farke. Furthermore, and adding to the disruption, several players had been forced into isolation from the training camp due to covid. This had resulted in a few of the warm-up games being cancelled.

The incomings did look very promising and included:

Milot Rashica and Josh Sargent (both from Werder Bremen in Germany), Angus Gunn (a pleasing return home from Southampton), Christos Tzolis, reunited with former teammate Dimitris Giannoulis (both PAOK in Greece), Ben Gibson (from Burnley – as with Giannoulis, his previous season loan deal now made permanent), Pierre Lees-Melou (from Nice in France) and finally, highly-rated youngster Billy Gilmour (on loan from Chelsea). A diverse mix of nationalities from different leagues who would surely require plenty of time, work and patience before they could settle, both on a professional and personal level.

The headline transfer out of the club had been last season's talisman and player of the year, Emi Buendia, for a club record and mouth-watering sale of £33 million (plus add-ons) to Aston Villa. It must always be pleasing for the selling club when Villa (or Newcastle United, for that matter) come in for a player as it appears that they are both willing to pay over the odds. You can imagine the conversation going something like:

Villa: "Hi Norwich. We'd like to sign Emi Buendia. Is he available for transfer?"

Norwich: "Yep. £25 million."

Villa: "Thanks! Is there any chance we can pay more as it would then look as though we are a bigger club than we actually are?"

Norwich: "Sure. Go for it."

In the morning's Pink Un football supplement to the Eastern Daily Press (EDP), Liverpool manager Jurgen Klopp praised Norwich's 'sensational' work in the transfer market. However, he ominously added that he preferred to have a calmer, more settled situation, keeping his team together for the long term with just the odd acquisition as and when required. This approach was typified with the inclusion in his squad of Premier League veteran of a staggering 20 years, James Milner, now in his 6th season for them.

Before leaving the Fat Cat, we had the privilege of seeing the owner Colin Keatley being presented with one of the 50 CAMRA (Campaign for Real Ale) Gold Awards. Launched this year to celebrate 50 years of campaigning, they were to honour the people, pubs, breweries and cider producers who have changed the face of the industry. The Fat Cat was pronounced by CAMRA as being 'a pub that has stood the test of time, convivial, characterful, community-focused and consistently pouring great pints' – a fitting accolade to a very popular City establishment much loved by drinkers from near and far.

It was now time to meet friend and fellow Norwich fan Paul in the Plough along St Benedict's Street. A robust six foot two and usually found proudly sporting his crochet yellow and green beanie hat; it's fair to say he has the capabilities of being the life and soul of any party. It's also fair to say he doesn't suffer fools gladly and it was this latter trait that had just surfaced.

"Kid, I won't be meeting you and Denise in the Plough as I've just had a 'barney' with them over their seating policy and told them to shove their ale."

"It'll have to be Plan B then," I thought and what an alternative it turned out to be…

Back in September 2019, before the home game with Manchester City, I had been contentedly sat in the Plough, nursing a pint of Grain Brewery Redwood – the calm before the sensational storm that was to conclude in a remarkable 3-2 victory for Norwich. Gazing through the window, not particularly watching people go about their business on what was a gloriously sunny afternoon, I was suddenly struck by the state of the building on the opposite side of the street; one that you couldn't help but notice due to its derelict appearance. St Benedict's Street (surprisingly the only such named street in the whole of Great Britain) houses an eclectic, extremely well-kept mix of coffee houses, licenced premises, music shops and, of course, the obligatory barbers and yet here was a building that stood out like a festering, sore thumb.

To my utter amazement, a lady then came out of the front door dressed in 1940s attire, complete with a cherry red headscarf and matching lipstick! "What the hell is that place across the road?" I probed the barmaid in the Plough.

"Not sure what goes on in there to be honest, as I've not been in yet, but I've been told it's some type of antique shop that also has a bar in the back. I believe it's called Arboretum although, again, I'm not totally sure as there are no signs up," she kindly informed me.

So, nearly two years later, I was walking past the Plough with Denise and Paul when they spotted that the door of this same, intriguing establishment was slightly ajar with a tantalising glimpse of what was contained inside. Denise asked the owner, who was crouched outside fussing his pet Irish Wolfhound, if it was OK to go in and have a look around. He pleasantly replied, "Of course, but before you do you need to know the one house rule that we have and that is, everything in the premises is for sale" before earnestly adding, "apart from me and the dog."

We tentatively crept in, unsure of what we were going to find, and were immediately transported into what had been transformed into someone's front room from a totally different era. It was purposely dimly lit, atmospheric and bizarrely comforting, swathed with curiosities with a 1940s soundtrack soothingly playing in the background. Had we stepped back in time? Had I imbibed too many pints of Green Jack Mahseer IPA in the Fat Cat?

Next, we stepped into the small, candlelit bar area, where we were asked if we would like to have drinks. Of course we would, we answered. Alarmingly, we were then seated in the outside area, which, at first glance, could only be described as being little more than a scrapyard with rickety old park benches and tables strewn around, surrounded by rusty saws, battered sewing machines and other such dilapidated items.

Thinking back to the owner's guidance that everything in the premises was for sale, I turned to Denise and Paul and, with raised eyebrows, whispered, "If anyone buys anything in here, other than the alcohol, they must be seriously deranged or extremely bladdered." Five minutes later, I was the proud owner of a 1930's Davall wall clock which only had a single hour hand, a scratched and scuffed surface, no glass and no pendulum - a bargain at eleven quid. The owner had initially wanted £15 as he cutely 'wasn't sure whether it was in working order or not'.

Arboretum (full name Arboretum Pharmaceutical Cocktail Services) is truly a unique Norwich venue that puts it outside of the traditional box of bar venues, defining their particular space away from that of other typical competitors. From not having any signage outside '*If the door is shut, check the candle in the lantern above the front door. If it is burning, we are serving'* to the apparently randomly strewn items (they're not; on closer inspection, you can appreciate that they have been strategically placed for effect) in the outside 'Salvage Yard'; this is an establishment that attracts a loyal customer base who are appreciative of the obvious work, effort and thought that has gone into it.

On my visit, they did have a good range of bottled beers from St Peters Brewery of Bungay but, according to online reviews, it is the 'old world' cocktails that most punters seek out, enjoy and, indeed, return for. I wonder how many of those are needed before you get the urge to buy a decrepit old clock?

Denise left us at this stage to check in at our 'digs' on Duke Street. It was now time for me and Paul to head to Carrow Road for the game, the match day atmosphere building as we got nearer to the ground. At the junction of Upper King Street/Prince of Wales Road, a large contingent of Liverpool fans, for some unfathomable reason, were staring up the road in a stunned silence towards Agricultural Hall Plain, as though they were witnessing the landing of a UFO.

Although there were large crowds congregating around the stadium, I made my way into the ground relatively easily, purchased a pie and predictably burnt my lip and the roof of my mouth.

I was now eager to make my way to my new seat, my new AISLE seat. Do you know where it was? Of course, it was in the middle of the row – another 'discussion' beckons with the ticket office, but that'll have to wait for now.

Just before kick-off, there was time for a spine-tingling

rendition of 'On The Ball City', the world's oldest football song. There was breath-taking (probably because I wasn't expecting them) pyrotechnics straggling the halfway line while yellow and green flags were vigorously and emotionally being waved by fans all around the Norwich sections of the ground – a marvellous spectacle.

Obviously buoyed by this support, once the whistle blew, City were in the game for large parts. There were reasonable early chances for Teemu Pukki and Lukas Rupp that were not converted and it didn't take long for Liverpool to capitalise. It ended harshly, in a 3-0 defeat, a spirited performance though that was good in parts. It didn't feel like the end of the world and there were plenty of reasons to be cheerful.

After the game, a bullish Daniel Farke said, "As long as we have that unity, I don't fear this league. I am sure we can have some beautiful moments together this season."

Klopp, meanwhile, sportingly acknowledged Norwich's tricky pre-season but also pointed out it was not too easy to face Liverpool anyway. He was happy with their performance and the result but thought they could play better.

Manchester City, Norwich's opponents next Saturday, will definitely be thinking the same after losing their opening game 1-0 to Tottenham...

Later on, all was calm in the city, with a mixture of football fans returning from the match mingling with the early evening patrons officially out on a session. All was calm, that was, apart from a well-dressed and somewhat harassed young lady who was apparently being given the run-around. On her mobile, standing outside the Wig &

Pen, she was blasting her date. "You told me you were in the Ribs, you weren't. Then you told me you were in the Louis, you weren't. Then you said the Wig, you aren't. Now you're telling me you're actually in the Red Lion! I can't keep searching around for you...I'm not a fucking helicopter!"

CHAPTER 2

LEICESTER CITY (H)

28TH AUGUST 2021

W e're just over a week into the new season and, according to certain pundits within the broadcast media, Norwich City's Premier League wagon has lost all of its wheels, with relegation a certainty already.

After the defeat to Liverpool the previous Saturday, Norwich had suffered a 0-5 humping at Manchester City - two games and two defeats against the last two champions of this unforgiving league.

It is true that it had been an awful weekend for the club overall, with a 0-1 defeat for the U23's against Stoke City plus a 0-10 battering at Aston Villa for the U18's also being encountered. Nonetheless, the mauling received afterwards from sports radio station Talksport was considered to be over the top.

The two main protagonists sticking their grubby boots in were Jamie O'Hara and Alex Crook. O'Hara had most recently been playing for Billericay Town in the National League South, where he had been in the news for leathering a Leatherhead fan after losing his cool after a defeat there. He'd also appeared in the 2017 series of Celebrity Big Brother. Crook, on the other hand, was billed as a newsman, presenter and commentator.

That neither of them possessed any expertise on the subject of Norwich City in general, and in particular, the far from ideal pre-season they had experienced, mattered not. O'Hara argued that the Premier League should revoke Norwich's membership, while Crook believed that they were cheating the system and that this went against sporting integrity.

Farke responded to this unjust criticism by saying, "If we are concerned with a 5-0 defeat at Manchester City, then we should not play at this level. We should stay at Championship level and congratulate ourselves every week."

He then hit the nail on the Talksport-shaped head by pointedly adding, "For me, it is not important at all if someone talks about us and they have not done their research. If someone says we don't have the right to play in the Premier League, we got 97 points in the Championship last season. Who else has done this? We earned our right to play at Premier League. We are a self-funding club, and we have earned more money than any club in Western Europe. I am not annoyed because sometimes you have to provoke to sell your news."

The unimaginative Crook, meanwhile, on Twitter, was revelling in his moment in the headlights of being the self-styled "public enemy number one among Norwich hall of famers" mockingly adding, "don't go into meltdown every time you get criticised."

Before the Leicester City fixture, Norwich had a home Carabao Cup game to play against last season's adversaries Bournemouth, who would be fielding their own wind-up merchant in Ben Pearson. Surely a role at Talksport alongside O'Hara and Crook beckons for him once his playing career is over?

Bournemouth, who had performed the 'double' over the Canaries last term, were no match this time for a rampant City team showing ten changes from the Manchester City game with only Lukas Rupp maintaining his place. With doubles from new signings Josh Sargent and Christos Tzolis, plus further strikes from Kenny McLean and Rupp, Norwich ran out comprehensive 6-0 winners.

Following the game, in the Norwich Evening News, a grounded Farke (and perhaps in response to a 'feast or famine' outlook from supporters) stated, "I am not over the moon in the same way I was not really disappointed at losing to two of the best sides in the world." He had savoured the evening though, and was relishing the selection issues for the weekend.

After travelling down by car to the Liverpool game, this was my first trip to the Fine City in a while on East Midlands Railways. I had received an e-mail from them in May informing me that new trains were in the pipeline (or should that be tunnel) on these regional routes with Class 170s set to replace the Class 15x fleet. There was no change this morning though.

Surprisingly and happily, there was a change to the timetable with a 07:54 having been added, a direct Chesterfield to Norwich service taking just 3 hours and 19 minutes, saving me over an hour on the usual Saturday morning pre-match journey.

Once on the train, there was also no change to the pre-covid behaviour of many of my fellow travellers as, with masks off, they heartily and happily coughed, sneezed, belched and farted indiscriminately. It's surely only a matter of time before the nation grinds to a halt with people suffering from coronavirus, chest infections, flu and distress of a gastrointestinal nature.

Today's pub of choice was the Duke of Wellington on Waterloo Road. Conveniently hosting their annual beer festival, there were over 30 (mainly northern) beers on offer to get us in the match day mood, all of which were dispensed from their glass-fronted tap room. My drinking buddies in attendance were life and soul Paul, dour and proud Yorkshireman Wiggy (now residing in Clungunford, Shropshire) and Alex (of Sheringham stock but now living in Leeds). Paul, a self-confessed drinker of the fizzy stuff, once promoted heavily by Australian breweries, mischievously questioned why pubs always had real ale festivals and not lager ones. "Cos lager's shite", retorted Wiggy with the facial expression of a man contemplating having to drink a half-pint of battery acid...or lager.

Arguably brought to real ale prominence by ex-landlord and local legend Dougie Clarke, the Duke (or Iron Duke as many locals refer to it due to the original pub name) is a friendly and welcoming hostelry with many nooks and crannies available in which to pass an hour or three.

As far back as the early 1930s, the building was home to Waterloo Stores, a corner shop with a bakery, plus a licence to sell alcohol. In 1937 it became the Iron Duke, a pub owned by Great Yarmouth brewery, Lacons. There are still a couple of physical nods on show towards this initial name, including the splendid pub signage above the front door plus the fading car park instructions attached to the side wall.

After further ownership changes to Whitbread and then Adnams, it became a freehouse in 2002 when the name changed to the current one. As well as having a fantastic beer garden comprising of more tables, a covered smoking area and an abundance of plants, possibly the main feature within the interior is a well-preserved, red brick, World War II air-raid shelter. This is visible on the walk-through to the toilets by way of a sheet of glass laid into the floor.

A quirk of the pub is that it has an entrance door that opens out onto the street and not into the premises, as is the norm of many public houses across the land. It's not surprising then, that many first-time visitors can think that the door is locked as the habit and general custom is to turn the handle, then push. A few years ago, I had arranged to meet a couple of Sheffield United-supporting friends here. From my place at the bar, and much to my amusement, I could see them walking to and fro past the pub windows looking perplexed. With increasing frustration at their attempts to gain entrance - as though they were appearing in their very own episode of the Crystal Maze - my phone predictably rang: "Mate, how the fuck do we get in?"

There is plenty of competition in this area of the City, with the Brewery Tap, Angel Gardens and Whalebone all in close proximity, plus the Artichoke, Kings Head and Plasterers slightly further afield. The Duke more than holds its own, however, and is justly acknowledged as being one of the City's premier real ale establishments.

After a splendid pre-match 'session' it was now game time, and I made my way to my AISLE seat in the middle of the row. On the Monday after the Liverpool game (and before my car journey back to Chesterfield), I had gone into the Norwich City Fan Hub on London Street, just down from the flagship department store and Norwich institution, Jarrolds. Incredibly, the official Carrow Road ticket office was now closed for in-person transactions, with the exception of first team home games, meaning any face-to-face contact must be within the Hub, which is described by the club as being 'much more than just a retail outlet'.

"Good morning. Can you help me with a season ticket issue that I have, please?"

"Of course, what is the issue?" was the polite and enthusiastic response.

"I asked for an aisle seat, but the ticket office sold me one that is in the middle of a row. Can I change this, please?"

"Ahhh, I'm afraid I can't help you with that. You need to phone the ticket office."

On returning home, I called the ticket office and asked the same question. Their response: "Ahhh, I'm afraid I can't help you with that. You need to send the ticket office an e-mail. Then we can look at your issue." She kindly provided me with the e-mail address.

Two weeks ago, I sent an e-mail – no answer, and followed this up with another one a week ago – no answer. Call me perceptive, but I've got a sneaky feeling that the blighters are giving me a swerve that Norwich midfielder

Kieran Dowell would be proud of. More on this fiasco later…

Today's opponents, Leicester City (nicknamed The Foxes), are the current holders of the FA Cup and the FA Community Shield. They had also finished 5th in the Premier League in both of the last two seasons and would surely be a formidable adversary. However, a quick glance on the supporter's message board 'Foxes Talk' indicated that some of their fan base were not totally happy with their lot and were, indeed, as fickle as any other club. This was after a 4-1 reverse at West Ham United, encountered earlier in the week. On a Norwich pre-match thread, negative comments were easy to come across, including:

"Expect Norwich to take the piss out of us, no defence, no width" and "Norwich have lost 12 Premier League games in a row without scoring…home win written all over it."

On the other hand, belligerent posts were also logged, such as:

"Norwich are useless and will be playing against players who are miles and miles ahead of them", plus "Could take West Ham United defeat out on Norwich/I think we will bounce back."

Once the game commenced, it seemed uncannily like the Liverpool game. There was a bright start from Norwich, who were, once again, cheered on by a vibrant, raucous home crowd. Unfortunately, just eight minutes in, an error from new loan signing Brandon Williams (plus a lack of adequate cover from his fellow defenders) resulted in Jamie Vardy unerringly rifling the ball past City keeper Tim Krul.

An all-too-easy, preventable concession and Leicester were in the ascendancy.

Norwich were handed a lifeline on the stroke of half-time from an unlikely ally; the Video Assistant Referee. Known to all and sundry as VAR, it had been no friend to the Canaries during their last season in the top flight. However, when Foxes defender Çaglar Söyüncü innocuously slid in to challenge Pierre Lees-Melou (with referee Robert Jones initially pointing for a corner), VAR checked the incident. After consulting the pitch-side monitor, Jones changed his original decision and awarded Norwich a penalty. "Fucking Eureka!" exclaimed the chap sitting to my right. I assumed this exaltation was because he was happy with the decision as my beady eye had not particularly noticed him invent anything during the previous 44 minutes. I must also confess to being relieved that he didn't totally channel his inner Archimedes and proceed to run around the streets undressed.

To the utter delight of the home faithful (obviously including my new Greek acquaintance), Teemu Pukki stepped up to the spot and confidently sent goalkeeper Schmeichel the wrong way for his, and the club's, first league goal of the season. 1-1, and the game was most certainly on.

Scoring opportunities for the hosts went begging throughout the second half, with Pukki, Sargent and Idah, in particular, all failing to convert acceptable chances. Meanwhile, in a rare visiting raid into Norwich territory, the previously innocuous Marc Albrighton put his team in the lead, albeit with a deflection off the lunging Williams. As with the first goal conceded, it appeared to happen all-too-easily.

There was still time for one last twist in the tale. Milot Rashica whipped in a corner that saw Kenny McLean jump head and shoulders above everyone else in the box to thump in a glorious header that we all thought was a deserved equaliser. The linesman had other ideas as he raised his flag to identify Todd Cantwell as straying offside smack in front of Schmeichel – a decision confirmed by VAR. "Get your flag down, you wanker", uttered a crestfallen 'Archimedes'.

Again, just like the Liverpool game, a spirited performance with much to admire. It had to be acknowledged though, that it was the third league defeat in succession. There was something that was just not right – similar to enjoying a curry at Ali Tandoori on Magdalen Street without the meal hitting any great heights due to the chef forgetting to (or being unable to) add that final, crucial spice that would make all the difference.

During his post-match press conference, Leicester boss Brendan Rodgers admitted that his team had not played well and yet (somehow) still managed to win. Regarding VAR, he thought the penalty decision could have gone either way but that the linesman/VAR combination had been correct to rule out McLean's header.

With all Premier League clubs now taking an enforced break due to international matches, there was only one team keeping Norwich off the foot of the table and that was Arsenal. The next fixture for the Canaries?...Arsenal (a) at the Emirates in two weeks' time.

CHAPTER 3

WATFORD (H)

18TH SEPTEMBER 2021

The summer transfer window finally closed on the 31st of August at 22:59 and we could all breathe a sigh of relief that none of the 'crown jewels' had been tempted away. If rumours were to be believed, unwanted late advances for fullbacks Max Aarons (from Borussia Dortmund) and Dimitris Giannoulis (from Roma) had swiftly, effectively and thankfully been rebuked by the club.

Also, two further incomings had been persuaded to join the Canary cause. Were these the final pieces of the jigsaw that Webber and Farke had been looking for; the final couple of 'spices' that needed adding to the recipe?

The first of the two to sign on the dotted line was 25-year-old Norwegian international, Mathias Normann, from Russian side FC Rostov. This was announced as a loan deal that would last until the end of the current season with an option, at the end, for Norwich to sign him on a permanent basis if all went well. A defensive midfielder with uncanny Action Man features, he seemingly relished the physical activity that had been missing in that position since ex-loanee Oliver Skipp had returned to his parent club, Spurs. Speaking to (official club website) Canaries.co.uk, Normann said, "I like to tackle, to win the ball and to use my body. I like to be on the ball and try to dictate the game."

The second, and final, new kid on the block was 21-year-old, 6ft 1in 'physically strong' central defender, Ozan Kabak. A highly-rated Turkish international signed from Schalke 04 FC in Germany, this was also a loan deal on the same terms as Normann. He had been on loan at Liverpool for the latter part of the previous season, where, according to Wikipedia, he had become the first Turkish player to appear for an English team in the Champions League. Significantly, this signing was a further impressive feather in Farke's Tirolerhut as Kabak had opted to sign for Norwich, amidst keen competition, due to the progress he felt he could make as a young player under the Head Coach's tutelage.

After Norwich had been relegated from the Premier League at the end of the 2019-2020 season, Stuart Webber had held up his hands and taken full responsibility, notably likening his lack of success in the transfer market to sending 'Daniel (Farke) to war without a gun'. The same could not be said this time around as, when the dust had settled after Kabak's arrival, 11 signings had been made, totalling approximately £50 million in cost. As the number of outgoings had unbelievably numbered 17, it must have felt like a mini-tornado had been propelled through the changing rooms and playing fields of the club's Colney training centre during the previous couple of months.

Around this time, an excellent, extremely informative

article by John Percy appeared in the Daily Telegraph, highlighting, in particular, a couple of the transfer deals. Buendia's sale to Aston Villa was classed as a whirlwind, with talks commencing on the 4th of June then, astonishingly, successfully concluding the following day. This was in comparison to the Kabak deal that Norwich were said to have worked on for a full six months. Six months! Crikey, in that time you could buy a house (from searching, to conveyancing - including signing and exchanging contracts - through to actually getting the keys), or commendably learn to dance, or (more pertinently), get through and then have a meaningful conversation with the ticket office at Norwich City FC.

OK, you've rumbled me. I made the last one up.

As they had still not responded to my e-mails, I attempted to call them again over the next few days to see if any progress had been made in regards to moving me from my phantom, pirate, ersatz AISLE seat to a real Elijah McCoy, full fat, bona-fide aisle seat (and yes, I've just had an absolute blast on the thesaurus).

1st attempt: "You are number 5 in the queue." That's not too bad, I thought; I'll be through in 10 minutes. Twenty-five minutes later, "You are number 5 in the queue." There was obviously a problem.

2nd attempt: I got straight through! "I can't help you with your issue as our system is down."

3rd attempt: After being "number 2 in the queue", I was swiftly through to an operator – then the call cut off.

Then finally, I got through and re-iterated my issue.

Ticket Office: "I'm sorry. We are not selling any more season tickets as we have reached our limit." In response, I explained that I didn't require an additional seat and that I just wanted to move my current one.

Ticket Office: "It's not possible to move you to another seat as all seats in the stadium have now been allocated for the season." I countered that this was not true as, by my reckoning, approximately two thousand tickets were available for purchase by club members on a match-by-match basis.

Ticket Office: "Well, I don't see what your problem is as, according to my seating plan, you are so obviously already in an aisle seat anyway." Oh…my…goodness. I took a deep breath and calmly began to explain that I had, so far, been to the Liverpool and Leicester games and that my seat was absolutely, categorically IN THE MIDDLE OF A ROW!

I then appealed to the clerk's empathetic nature. "Can you just imagine, for one moment, going into a shop and buying an item for £500. Before you actually get to check the item, the shop wraps it up for you. When you get home, you find they have given you the wrong item. What would you do given that situation?"

A penny dropped, and she went off to investigate. On her return, I had miraculously been allocated a new seat which was most definitely, I was assured, an aisle seat.

So, there we have it. Just like that. After a full 14 months of trying, I finally have what I wanted. In the same time, I could have been on my way to purchasing a third house, been proficient enough in dance to enable me to enter competitions in Blackpool, while City could have engaged in more than a couple of Ozan Kabak-length transfer deals.

"Be careful, though", warned the delectable Denise. "You could now be sat next to one of those obnoxious-type fans who know it all." Talk about raining on my yellow and green parade...

As the international break drew to a close, the 15 senior players who had been on representative duty began to filter back to what must have been a rather deserted Colney training centre during the previous fortnight. As some of them were not due to arrive back until late on Thursday evening, this was giving Farke hardly any time at all to prepare for the upcoming game at Arsenal. Add in the fact that some had featured in 3 games during the past week, no doubt picking up bumps and bruises along the way, not to even mention travel fatigue; it would be a herculean task for him to gel a competitive outfit together.

In the end, there were four changes made to the team that had faced Leicester, including Christos Tzolis and the strapping 6ft 2in central defender, Andrew Omobamidele – a proud moment for the two 19-year-olds who would be making their Premier League debuts. Omobamidele, in particular, was experiencing a meteoric rise to the elite levels of professional football, having only made his first-team (Championship) debut as recently as the 2nd of April this year, against Preston North End. Furthermore, during the latest round of internationals, he'd also been handed his first cap by the Republic of Ireland.

Ultimately, the Arsenal game (which was the charismatic Farke's 200th in charge of the Canaries) was decided by a Pierre-Emerick Aubameyang tap-in that looked for all the world, both in real-time and playback, like he was offside.

Ex-official Chris Foy was a man who had always possessed that special, intrinsic, almost organic quality of being able to fuck up any game, anytime, anywhere due to his refereeing inadequacies. He was that bad he had often had both managers (and both sets of fans) united in bemoaning his performance - quite the accolade. He was also well known for having a constant puzzled look on his face as though one of the players had asked him a particularly tricky maths question such as "Hey Chris. Did you know that 7 out of 5 people can't do fractions?"

He was now to be found trying to explain crucial decisions in the Mail on Sunday, where he is rather remarkably masquerading as an 'expert'. Here's what he thought of the Gunners winner: "THIS was a straightforward decision, and it was the right outcome. When Nicolas Pepe shoots initially, Pierre-Emerick Aubameyang is in an offside position — but this isn't an offence. Tim Krul then saves the shot; the ball deflects off Pepe and falls to Aubameyang. However, he is behind the ball when it hits Pepe, so he can't be offside. A factual and completely correct decision."

We'll have to beg to differ then Foy because whatever way I looked through my green and yellow-tinted spectacles, he was offside. Also, I had a nagging feeling that if this had been at the 'other end', we may well have seen the goal disallowed.

Daniel Farke, asked for his view on the goal after the game by Pink Un reporter Paddy Davitt, was far more diplomatic in his response. He had not watched the footage, did not want to watch the footage and accepted the decision to award the goal.

He now had the luxury of a full week to work with his players on how to beat the next opponent, Watford. It was not exactly panic stations, but (stating the bleedin' obvious) City clearly needed to start getting points on the board sooner rather than later. Chris Sutton, ex-Norwich forward, speaking on the BBC Five Live 'Monday Night Club' the previous week, raised a concern that had probably crossed most supporters' minds. He said, "I'm worried about the effect the start could have on the players and their confidence." We'll all have to see how this manifests itself over the coming weeks...

As you approach the Wig & Pen with your back to the resplendent Church of England Cathedral, it looks both welcoming and enticing in a comforting way – think about the first bite of a slice of cheese on toast, putting on your favourite pair of slippers, or in my case, having my first Watford pre-match beer of the day.

The building, dating back to the 17th century, is believed to have become a public house during the 1760s with the initial name of The White Lion. The current name was adopted in 1985 with a nod to the nearby Magistrates Court.

Since buying the freehold from Grand Metropolitan as long ago as 1993, affable owner Craig McLaren has had the pub in the palm of his hand. He remembers plenty of work that needed doing in his early days here, in particular, serious structural problems that were as a result of a mid-1980s redevelopment-gone-wrong. Once these had been rectified though, the pub soon began to attract a loyal customer base from workers at the adjacent Bussey's Garage plus staff from Jarrold's Printing Works, who were based just around the corner on Fishergate. Old football teammates of Craig's were also regular punters in the early days (and most still are some 28 years later). In my mind, I can see him in his prime as having been a robust, enthusiastic stopper in the Malky McKay mould, but he assures me that he was actually a fleet-footed striker like Chris Sutton – I'll have to take his word on that.

Interestingly, and bearing in mind that Grand Metropolitan had sold the freehold in the belief that the pub wasn't economically viable, Craig had a rock-solid contingency if all had not gone to plan. The building would be converted into two attractive townhouses – evidence of his pre-licenced trade days in the construction industry plus his strong business acumen showing through here.

Having taken initial inspiration from the Ribs of Beef next to Fye Bridge, he has always had real ale on the menu, with a couple of his early offerings being Boddingtons and Woodfordes. As the beers are usually dispensed in tip-top condition, well-deserved awards have followed, with the 'Wig' being consistently in the CAMRA Good Beer Guide over the past 20 years, plus the added honour of being a former recipient of the East Anglian Pub of the Year Award. Also, although not an award, it is an intriguing fact that in 1995 the 'Wig' was the first pub in Norwich to be granted a Tables & Chairs Licence. I wonder how many of these licences have been applied for in the City since by not only bars but restaurants and cafes as well, particularly during covid times when only an outdoor service could be provided.

Remember those early-days customers from Jarrold's Printing Works? Well, they were involved in a rumpus that Craig still recalls clearly to this day. In 1996, Jarrold's were investing in new printing machines from Germany. As part of the deal, they were being installed by German engineers at a time when England was gripped with the national football team's efforts to get to the final of Euro96. During the early stages of the competition, all had been well in the pub, with both German and English colleagues watching the football in a convivial atmosphere. That was until the semi-final, of course, when Craig remembers all hell breaking loose after the infamous penalty shoot-out that resulted in England being knocked out! Anglo-German relations were happily soon restored though, after a diplomatic intervention from the Landlord.

Fast forward to Monday the 22nd of January 2001, and it's the day of long-serving Norwich City physiotherapist Tim Sheppard's well-deserved testimonial game against Scottish powerhouse Glasgow Celtic, managed at the time by ex-City player and manager Martin O'Neill (with the previously mentioned former City and now Celtic attacker Chris Sutton prominent on the cover of the match day programme). It's early afternoon, and Craig is overseeing a tranquil lunchtime session consisting of a few diners and a smattering of regulars enjoying a pint while doing the crossword. Imagine the look on self-confessed Glasgow Rangers fan Craig's face as he looks through the window to see two coach loads of boisterous and very thirsty Celtic supporters descending on his pub. After a few hours of mayhem, Craig revealed the marauding visitors had indeed, "drunk him dry" – they had also relieved him of all of the pub's Bric-a-Brac! For the record, 'CelticWiki' recounted that there had been an impressive 5,000 Celts in a crowd of 15,034 and had 'earned plaudits for their behaviour'.

As he is now fast approaching his pearl anniversary at

the pub, I wonder how much longer Craig has left at the helm. Well, for all patrons with a requirement for stability, continuity, reliability, familiarity and quality (including the healthy number of City fans who use this pub as their match day base), there is good news. Craig has confirmed that he has no immediate plans to vacate the premises as he has acknowledged that he would miss the day-to-day hands-on involvement with the pub far too much.

Today, I'm sat outside on the Wig's terrace, explaining to life and soul Paul in great detail why I think it will be extremely difficult for Norwich to get a positive result against Watford. In what is an epic monologue, I elaborate on all the issues (new signings finding their feet, players released, covid repercussions, international call-ups, injuries) and can't fail to notice that his eyes have glazed over. He is certainly making an effort to stay awake though, nodding at key moments to assure me he is keeping up and possibly agreeing with me? There's not a chance of the latter when he responds, "Load of bollocks kid. We'll muller 'em 4-0!"

We then find out that Farke has rung the changes once more with five players coming into the team who did not start the previous game at Arsenal. For some reason, this is a cause for optimism amongst most of my fellow fans before kick-off. Alternatively, I have a nagging feeling there may be trouble ahead as the chosen defence is, once again, changed and totally lopsided, with all four of them predominantly right footed. Last season there was a huge fanfare emanating from the club when they addressed the 'balance' issues of the back-line with the signings of left-footed left-back Giannoulis and left-footed centre-back

Gibson. This would appear not to be a current priority, with Grant Hanley and Brandon Williams being the unfortunate players - both selected in positions where they are not entirely comfortable.

For a match report, you may well want to refer to my accounts of the previous two home games, i.e. a bright start by the Canaries roared on by a boisterous crowd only for it all to fall apart after some dozy defending. Talk about Groundhog Day; all we were missing was a furry animal, a grumpy meteorologist, plus Sonny and Cher serenading us with 'I got you, babe'.

Pukki, as in the Leicester game, drew City level before the break with a superb trademark finish (or should that be Finnish) before further errors in the second half from the beleaguered back four gave Watford the helping hand they needed to cement a 3-1 victory. Disturbingly, after the third goal, we witnessed several players conducting a very public inquest, pointing 'the finger of blame' at colleagues, followed by a slumping of the shoulders and a bowing of the heads. With 10 minutes left on the clock, it looked like they had given up, as had a lot of fans, with many heading for the exits. At least they were spared the delirious visiting supporters joyously dipping into their songbook that could have been entitled 'Now that's what I call piss-take football chants'. At the final whistle, several 'boos' were audible.

Before the 17:50 train home, I met up with Sheffield-based and long-time friend Richard in the Coach and Horses on Thorpe Road for the post-match analysis, a swift couple of pints of rejuvenating Chalk Hill Brewery Gold, and most essentially, chilli and chips. As we were pushed for time, Richard enquired what the waiting time was for food. The barman, with a face as expressionless as one of the lamp posts outside the pub entrance, informed him, "Well, you could get served about twenty to six…, but it could be earlier…or later." With indecision like that, it could only be a matter of time before Stuart Webber signs him on loan for the rest of the season (obviously with a view to signing him permanently) to play in City's defence.

Speaking to the local media on the Monday after the game, a very candid Farke reported, "We had a team meeting to analyse, to be self-critical, to be honest. We have to improve our defending behaviour; we concede too many goals at the moment. We cannot hide behind the fact on this topic, we are not good enough. We spoke as well about the reaction after the third goal. I do not want to see that again. Now we are in a much better mood and ready to go."

Sensationally, he then added, "I would like to announce we are making every effort to sign an out-of-contract defender who's been working behind the bar recently at a nearby hostelry. He is greedy to add to the hesitancy."

OK, once again, you've rumbled me. I could have made the last bit up.

CHAPTER 4

BRIGHTON & HOVE ALBION (H)

16TH OCTOBER 2021

Three days after the Watford defeat, Liverpool made a swift return to Carrow Road, this time for a Carabao Cup 3rd round tie. Not only did Farke make a hefty nine changes to Saturday's line-up, but he also switched to a formation (for the first time this season) that featured three central defenders in a bold move that would hopefully see his side improve their 'defending behaviour'. Perhaps unsurprisingly, given the combination of these alterations plus the standard of the opposition, Norwich were a goal down after 4 minutes – different formation, different personnel, same result. Two further soft goals were conceded after the halftime break gifting the away side another 3-0 victory.

Once again, things could have been so much different had City converted a spot-kick while they were still only 0-1 down. Instead, we were subjected to the bizarre pre-penalty spectacle of the nominated taker, Adam Idah, having the ball snatched out of his hands by an all too eager Christos

Tzolis. I'm not sure of the statistics on these situations – no doubt someone will be - but my gut feeling, at that moment, suggested that the Greek international was much more likely not to score, and disappointingly this was the outcome. It was a poor penalty by any standards; nothing more than a pass-back down the middle of the goal. Liverpool goalkeeper, Caoimhín Kelleher, did his best to dive out of the way and spare Tzolis's blushes, but right at the last minute, he stuck out a leg to divert the ball to safety.

Ultimately, when the full-time whistle blew, nobody had held their hand up for selection in the team for the next league game at Everton, which Norwich again lost, this time 2-0. There were another eight changes to the Carabao Cup line-up, although the back three formation was retained. In general, the defensive performance was more solid, although this possibly had an impact on creative output as there was little threat up front.

On the Monday after this latest reverse, I decided to listen (via playback) to the fan's phone-in programme, Canary Call, that was initially aired on BBC Radio Norfolk immediately after the game at Goodison Park. Hosted by self-confessed 'fan with a mike' Rob Butler, the time-honoured tradition is that if Norwich win then there are a wealth of acclaims while, on the other hand, a defeat is followed by a 60 minute moan fest. Curiously, it's a rarity for any of the callers to have actually attended the match, which they are prepared and eager to give an 'informed' account of.

Rob knows what's coming as he's "got a feeling the old lines will be busy again tonight", and this immediately proves to be correct. First on, there's Anna; she's not sure where the problem lies with the performances, but she would love to know "what's going on in training."

Next up, we have Tony, who is not happy with the manager for changing the formation. All pretty standard comments so far, following an away defeat. There's not been any need for Rob to get involved yet, although experience has taught him not to stoke a situation unnecessarily anyway, preferring to keep the middle ground in a tried and tested format.

Then Benjamin's on the line. He's done his homework and has a plethora of statistics on hand to slaughter Daniel Farke with (although unacceptably, he doesn't appear to have one that confirms how many Greek internationals have successfully converted a penalty after snatching the ball out of the hands of the nominated taker). "Stats don't lie, lads...stats don't lie." He's certainly passionate, almost preaching to convince us that he is right. "Stats don't lie... lads, stats don't lie."

The most pertinent and damning one (for him anyway) is that City have now lost their last 16 Premier League games. The fact that 10 of those defeats were at the back-end of the 2019-2020 season – and we've had a Championship-winning campaign since – cuts no ice with Benjamin. The common denominator is Farke and, just in case we've forgotten, "the stats don't lie." He's not interested in covid, a lack of a decent pre-season and new signings yet to settle in.

It's all gloom and doom from the callers so far, but then, for the first time, there's a hint of positivity in the shape of a Tim Krul post-match interview. The City custodian concedes that the new players still need to gel but nevertheless acknowledges that the team still need to find a way to win. He still believes that the situation will turn though "for sure."

Finally, we hear from a breath of fresh air called Linda, who's fed up with all the negativity. In my view, she raises the most valid point of the show. She reminds us all that it took a while for players to get used to Farke's formation and playing style when he first came into the club in 2017, and that is the same issue now with the influx of new signings – she's confident the situation will surely improve.

As the programme draws to a close, Rob's done well. We've had two out of the three topics raised that are expected during a disappointing run, i.e. (1) what's going on in training and (2) the manager getting some stick. The only one missing for a Canary Call hat-trick is (3) no one has called for Delia and Michael to be 'sacked'. He's not had to hit any great heights, but then again, he's not really had an opportunity to. It's been a steady Max Aarons-type 7/10 performance. He's let the callers have their say and then graciously and genuinely thanked them for phoning in and contributing, but it can't be easy for him hosting the show every week while his team continues to lose.

A general problem for Rob on Canary Call is that he has just the one football team to take calls on and discuss. Compare this to other local phone-ins such as 'Praise or Grumble' on BBC Radio Sheffield. Here they have fans of Sheffield United, Sheffield Wednesday, Chesterfield, Rotherham, Barnsley and Doncaster all vying for attention and air time, not only eager to comment on that afternoon's performances but also tearing strips off each other with historical subplots and wind-ups.

Rob does not have the luxury of this variety to ease him through his show, although it must be more enjoyable for him to take the calls after a win or, indeed, during a title-winning campaign. It's certainly more pleasurable to listen to. My mind goes back to the heady days of May earlier in the year after Norwich had lifted the Championship trophy on the pitch at Oakwell after the 2-2 draw against Barnsley. On that memorable afternoon, one of the show's inimitable and best-loved characters phoned in – Psychic Sandra. She endearingly and gleefully informed us all that every year on her birthday, her brother gives her some money in an envelope. She then takes the money to her local bookies and puts it on Norwich to finish in a certain position the following season and, more often than not, she ends up winning. I'm certain I'm not on my own when I say that I sincerely hope that she wins this season as she confesses she has them finishing in 10th spot in the Premier League. We're all rooting for you, Sandra!

Later, on the same day that I listened to Canary Call, I noticed that Rob's Radio Norfolk colleague (and esteemed Norwich City match-day commentator) Chris Goreham, has also tapped into the available glut of statistics in his weekly Eastern Daily Press column. Apparently, it's the first time Norwich have ever lost the first six games of a season; in fact, they had never lost the first five before this one. If "stats don't lie" Benjamin is aware of this, I can visualise him enthusiastically cartwheeling around his neighbourhood, throwing in the odd triple Salchow, with pike, for good measure...hopefully in a Captain Canary costume.

Chris initially questions if this latest statistic indicates that this is the worst team to ever wear yellow and green before acknowledging that 'there is more to football than numbers'. Exactly this, Chris. Just as Aaron Levenstein (a former Business Professor at Baruch College, New York) once famously elucidated, "Statistics are like bikinis. What they reveal is suggestive, but what they conceal is vital."

A week after the Everton fixture, the City faithful were back on the laborious five-hour trek to the north-west, this time to visit Burnley. For this journey, many would have been astutely bedecked in waterproofs, goloshes, and maybe even a green and yellow snorkel. Just as us Norwich fans tire at the lazy comments about our club, notably relating to Delia and cooking (blah blah blah), I'm sure that our Burnley counterparts despair at their association with inclement weather conditions constantly enveloping their town. Not as if they're particularly bothered by the elements, though, judging by how many wander around in the rain in their short-sleeved replica claret & blue tops, seemingly oblivious to the general wetness.

According to Wikipedia, the town's name is believed to have derived from Brun Lea, meaning 'meadow by the River Brun'. It is, therefore, completely logical that in the year 1251, the official name was actually 'Brunley' (note where the letter 'r' is placed), although 'Brunlea' would possibly have been more appropriate. What is absolutely fascinating is that someone, somewhere, at some time, decided it would be a great idea to move the 'r' after the 'u'. What on earth? I guess we should consider ourselves fortunate that some (feasibly) underworked city council clerk back in medieval days (bird-quill ink pen suspended over parchment) didn't have the not-so-bright candle-lit idea of changing the name of the Fine City to Nowrich. Just imagine the lazy headlines we could be subjected to, for example," Now rich Delia's City cook up a feast with Premier League parachute payments"...or something along those lines.

Over the 90 minutes, Norwich deserved their first point of the season after the 0-0 draw (the first time in 44 meetings the fixture had ended with this score-line). They had their chances with the impressive Normann, firstly drawing a fine save from Nick Pope from a free-kick, then clipping the bar later on after a mesmeric run that saw him slalom around some bewildered Burnley defenders.

The home side were aggrieved not to have been awarded a spot-kick after Krul decked striker Matej Vydra with a punch that former Norwich world boxing champ Jon Thaxton would have been proud of. According to the Burnley Express, he was winded and struggling for breath, having to be replaced before halftime. Referee Friend and VAR were in agreement, though – no penalty. Gravelly–voiced Clarets boss, Sean Dyche was not happy. Speaking to 'Lancs Live' he grumbled, "Our record of penalties is horrendous; everyone knows that. It is very difficult it seems, for us to get a penalty; we have to get absolute stonewallers where everyone in the stadium can see it." He thought the referee's performance was "indifferent."

As the second international break of the season came into view, Norwich City's travelling support was more than happy to be heading back east, initially through the northwest puddles, with a precious point. A difficult obstacle had been surmounted; a challenging bridge crossed. As the Seagulls of Brighton hover on the horizon in a fortnight, could that elusive first win finally be in sight?

Brighton are no mugs this season, which is their 5th back in the big-time following promotion four seasons ago. After four finishes, all between 15th and 17th, they are now rather impressively sat in 6th position in the fledgling table: just the one defeat (a home reverse, 0-2 v Everton) and undefeated away. They have developed a penchant for netting late goals with a 90th-minute winner from Leandro Trossard at Brentford plus a 95th-minute equaliser from niggly Neal Maupay at Crystal Palace. We've seen Neal the Niggle before at Carrow Road in October 2018 when (playing for previous club Brentford) he gloriously smashed the ball against the crossbar and over from 3 yards out – a crucial miss with City going on to win a tight game 1-0.

Ahead of the fixture, Brighton boss Graham Potter was realistic when assessing his team's start. He thought that not much was actually different from last season apart from they had probably had more good luck so far – or there had perhaps been an absence of bad luck.

On the eve of the game, I decided to pay my first visit to the Malt & Mardle on Magdalen Street. When I first had a chat with Elliot Dransfield (who is one of the three co-owners) during May earlier in the year, I was surprised to learn that it was to become the first micropub in Norwich, with a proposed opening date of 21 June 2021. I say surprising as the City is usually at the forefront of the UK's real ale activities, but not in the micropub category where many others have been successfully trading for a while, for example, in North Walsham, Cromer and over in the far west of the county in King's Lynn.

Elliot and the other two co-owners, Emily and Johnny, having already acquired a mutual love of cask and craft ales in the excellent Leeds hostelries of Whitelock's Ale House, Foleys Tap House, Friends of Ham and Brudenell Social Club, were inspired to ultimately open their own real ale emporium in Norwich on their return to the City after studying at the University of Leeds.

I considered the chosen location for the Malt & Mardle at the northern end of Magdalen Street to be an inspired decision. Not only is there much brewery and pub history associated with this lively thoroughfare (there has been at least 15 pubs on the street from one time to another), it is just a mere 100 feet to the magnificent City Walls (passing the imaginatively titled Wall Lane) and in particular, what used to be the site of the Magdalen Gates. Making full use of the local building material, flint with brick and stone reinforcements, work started on the walls in 1294 and was more or less completed by 1320. Originally forming the longest circuit of urban defences in Britain, eclipsing even those of London, to date, quite a lot of the structure still remains around the City, with much of Norwich's medieval past visible. Personally, I've always been fascinated with them and am sure that if they were elsewhere, these walls would be feted much more than they are in Norwich. Here though, it's as though they are just, well…there, lost in plain sight. In a strange sort of way, they're comparable with the most easterly point of the mainland, Ness Point in nearby Lowestoft, where, unlike the other UK extremities, there is nothing to celebrate the landmark other than a big compass dial. Maybe the respective Council(s) are missing a trick to pull in visitors and much-needed custom? Elliot himself confesses that it was not the historical aspect that had initially attracted him to the premises; it was just that he had spotted them as being vacant during an afternoon cycle ride and that a combination of the suitability of size, the general cost and the agreement of the landlord that a micropub could operate here had been his main reasons.

The main selling point of the Malt & Mardle is the constant rotation of four ales (two cask & two keg) with refrigerated craft beers for sale in the form of cans. There are other drinks to entice punters in, such as wine and gin etc., but with a total floor space of 334 square feet, in common with other micropubs, there is simply not enough room to stock the number of products that a traditional pub is able to. What we can be guaranteed of though, is the quality of the ales – Elliot is definitely passionate about the subject and, of course, would only be prepared to provide what he would want to drink himself. I wish him and his partners all the very best in this venture of adding another piece to the rich real ale tapestry of the City.

At the same time as I had an initial chat with Elliot, I noticed that the Canaries had confirmed their first signing since winning the Championship. It was Kenny Coker, a 17-year-old striker from Southend United who had impressed the club after a short trial. He'd actually made five first team appearances for The Shrimpers, but it was thought that he would start his Norwich career in the Academy. When asked for his thoughts on why City had been attracted to Coker, his Academy Manager at Southend, Ricky Duncan, thought it was because 'He's something that they (Norwich) don't have'. As with the new micropub, I thought it would be intriguing to see how they both develop in the future.

I'm pleased to report that the 'chic and charming' Malt & Mardle has started off very well. Quality local products (specifically relating to the cask, cider and bottled beer offerings) are on sale for customers appreciative of the cosy and friendly vibe. On the other hand, Kenny Coker has had somewhat of a mixed start to life in a struggling Norwich U18 team. At the time of writing, he'd made three starts (with one substitute appearance) and had not appeared in the last couple of games since scoring a consolation penalty against Brighton. More on these two later...

Remember the miracle of me being allocated a new seat which was most definitely an AISLE seat? Well, I was so excited at the thought of acquainting myself with it that I went into the ground extra early (10 to 3-ish, I know, I know – commitment, hey?), actually foregoing my last pre-match pint! I briskly walked through the concourse, not exactly at race pace but not far off, to the stand entrance. The sharp smell of the freshly cut grass filled my nostrils; Kasabian boomed out of the tannoy into my ears. It's always Kasabian, isn't it? That one song seemingly playing on loop, match after match. I swear you can walk past Carrow Road at 3:30 a.m., and it'll still be playing – just that one song. My eyes eagerly scanned the weather faded yellow seating. I located my row, taking a note that the seat next to that particular aisle was numbered 319, a mere ten away from mine. I followed the numbering across the line to my seat, my new AISLE seat. Well, IT'S NEXT TO A FUCKING WALL. I kid you not. Yet another 'discussion' beckons with my friends in the ticket office.

This did not bother me too much though against our visitors from the south coast. Yes, it was another 0-0 draw (the first home point gained this season), but it somehow felt like so much more. Judging from the reactions from the home faithful, many thought the same as me, particularly during the second half, as spontaneous and heart-lifting renderings of 'On The Ball City', 'Come on you Yellows' and 'Come on City' rang out around a vibrant Carrow Road. You've got to have hope in your hearts, haven't you?

The elusive winner didn't materialise as Josh Sargent missed the best chance of them all when presented with an open goal from 20 yards out. His effort totally lacked power allowing Brighton defender Shane Duffy to cover around and comfortably clear the danger. Teemu Pukki will also feel he could've done better as well, managing to dink the ball over Spanish goalkeeper Robert Sanchez but the wrong side of the post.

Neal Maupay (my latest pantomime villain) added to the atmosphere by constantly kicking the ball away, throwing the ball away, standing in the way at free kicks and niggling away at the referee throughout the 90 minutes. This was all undertaken in a crafty and subtle manner, thus avoiding a yellow card - 'nigglyness' of the highest order. How we laughed then when he had Brighton's best chance towards the end of the game. Just like the already mentioned Brentford match three years prior, he was presented with another sitter from 3 yards out, but this time, instead of smashing the ball against the crossbar and over, he cleared the bar completely.

The result meant the Canaries were still perched on the bottom rung while the Seagulls had soared up to a heady fourth place. Speaking to BBC Sport, Farke was "A bit disappointed that we didn't get all three points, but we did a lot of things; getting off the mark at home, backing up the draw at Burnley, creating more chances and keeping another clean sheet. It is the next step. You always want to take a big step, but you have to take what you can at this level. We are not dancing on the table; it is only a point. The final piece was missing. But it is a step in the right direction."

Potter, meanwhile, felt "It was a hard-fought game. We weren't at our best but not too bad either, and in the end, after both teams had chances, we accept the point." Intriguingly, fan site 'We are Brighton' suggested that not all of their supporters were as accepting after reporting that a scuffle had broken out in the away section just after the final whistle. Apparently, the argument started when someone claimed 'Brighton should be beating teams like Norwich' and their failure to do so meant they didn't deserve to be clapped off.

CHAPTER 5
LEEDS UNITED (H)
31ST OCTOBER 2021

I once knew a pub landlord who ran a local hostelry (one I rarely frequented, I must add). When I asked him if he enjoyed his job, he answered sincerely, "It's OK apart from when some customers come through the door and, before they've even reached the bar, you want to knock their heads off." I was slightly bemused with the response; surely a pub landlord should expect (and financially benefit from) having patrons in his pub?

I also knew a personal trainer who finished her stint in a local sports club because she was "fed up dealing with sweaty people at the gym." Similarly to my reaction as above, I was perplexed that a personal trainer would view a perspiring customer in a gym as undesirable.

I do wonder if it is this type of mentality that engulfs the employees at the Norwich City ticket office – not all of them, but definitely some. I can imagine them getting home in the evening and their partner asking if they have had a good day. "Well, it would have been OK, but we kept getting bothered by people ringing up for match tickets - fools, the lot of 'em!"

On the Monday before the upcoming fixture at Chelsea, I call and get through to a ticket office stalwart who doesn't suffer us 'fools' gladly. He's not as brusque as he was when he first started his role there, but I can't imagine in what universe he'd ever get nominated for an award in customer excellence. I begin by telling him about my predicament (i.e. that I was promised an aisle seat back in July 2020, I like the Wensum area of the main stand as it's ideal for a quick entry & exit, no stairs, easy access to the facilities and so on...) but don't get very far beyond 'was promised an aisle seat' before he stops me with what sounds like a snort of derision. "Look, you're not going to get an aisle seat in that area. What you're asking for is something that isn't there, unless you want me to get you one with a restricted view. I can get you one in the Regency, I can get you one in the Jarrold, I can even get you one in the Lower Barclay, but there's nothing in the Wensum." I ask him if he's sure and, after a second disdainful snuffle, he confirms he is absolutely certain before adding, "There is another option. Just have a look around you on a match day and if you see an empty aisle seat, just go and sit in it."

He then finished off by asking, "Is there anything else I can help you with?"

Well, I can't say that I'd realised he'd helped me with anything anyway, although at least I definitely know now that there are no suitable aisle seats available in my chosen area. That, however, would have been better to know a while ago and would have prevented me from pissing in the wind for the best part of 15 months. The pause button has now been pressed in my quest. As a parting shot, I mentioned to him that I would try again in May when the club operate a 'movers & shakers' period – enabling season ticket holders to change their seats if required. I then notice him exhale forcibly (for the third time) before he replies, almost mockingly, "Yeah, you could try that if you want."

On a positive note, there was splendid news from Chelsea ahead of Norwich's visit to Stamford Bridge when they announced that star strikers Romelu Lukaku and Timo Werner were both unavailable for the game. We should have known not to be too excited at this as Blues boss Thomas Tuchel (a close friend of Farke) just asked a couple of his young tyros, namely Mason Mount and Callum Hudson-Odoi, to solve the striking crisis, saying it was their opportunity to 'step up'. They duly obliged, both scoring in the opening 18 minutes, putting Chelsea into an early and ultimately unassailable 2-0 lead. Mount (scoring his first Chelsea goals since netting in the Champions League semi-final second leg win against Real Madrid in May) finished the game with a hat-trick as the Canaries were well and truly walloped 0-7.

Ex-City striker Dean Ashton was the latest Talksport employee to 'slam' his former club, although this time, you genuinely got the feeling he was hurting as much as the fans, not just taking the usual cheap shots preferred by some of his colleagues. He pulled no punches with his after-match views. "Sorry, Norwich, but it's just abysmal defending. If you don't get close to quality players, you're going to get punished. Rudiger all of a sudden looks like Cafu on the right-hand side."

"They're making good players look like incredible

players. They're allowing Chelsea to have five or ten yards of space and it's making themselves feel and look like they're Messi-esque. There were 'olés' from the Chelsea fans. Chelsea were good, absolutely; they've got quality players, but I'm sorry, I just don't recognise this Norwich team."

"I'm embarrassed to watch that, and Norwich fans should be too. It was a woeful performance to just allow Chelsea to show off. It was painful to watch."

Rob Butler's also straight on it after the game via his Facebook page with four simple but very effective lines:

Chelsea 7 (seven) Norwich 0

Dear oh dear

Farke is under real pressure from the fans...

It's a low point. It really is.

By the end of the day, he's attracted a host of comments from City fans in response. The prize for best remark (inadvertent or not) has to go to a Christopher Benton, who classes the performance as 'shambollock'. I think we know what he's trying to say, but he's possibly nailed it better than he ever intended.

Many of the responses (although most certainly not all) are demanding change within the club's hierarchy, although how and when this is supposed to occur is generally unclear. Change can be hard but admitting that change is required is sometimes even harder, depending on how firmly we have entrenched our position/view and to whom. Who at the club is ultimately responsible for shining a different light? Is it Delia and Michael on Webber, or Delia, Michael and Webber on Farke, or just Webber on Farke? However, change happens. It is ultimately uncomfortable for some and yet utterly liberating for others. One thing is for sure; change at some stage is inevitable, even in things we hold most sacred that we find hard to imagine altering at all. For example, Farke only signed a new four-year contract in July and looked to be embedded in his role as Head Coach until 2025. Yet after the debacle at Chelsea (typified by his players demonstrating a total lack of the general basic traits that fans view as a 'given' such as tracking back, closing down, supporting teammates, aggression, effort etc.), his position did not look anywhere near as secure from the fans perspective as it had just a mere three months prior.

Norwich now have a run of four fixtures within the next month that includes three games at Carrow Road, the place Farke often relates to as 'our living room'. He will not be alone in wanting and needing a decent points haul from these, commencing with the visit from the Peacocks of Leeds United (who are also struggling at the wrong end of the table) in a game to be televised on Sky TV on Sunday with a 2 p.m. start time.

Three days before the fixture, we get a rare chance to hear from Sporting Director Stuart Webber, who makes an impassioned plea to the Canary faithful to not give up on the team. He acknowledges the dismal points return and the dire position in the table but nevertheless reiterates that this is not the time for everybody to give up and that we all need to come together and 'show some teeth'. He confirms that the Head Coach is not under any threat of losing his job as it's not right to point the finger at just one person – everyone in the club needs to step up. It's evident that he believes there is a good chance of getting out of the current situation, but they do need to start winning games and to 'come out fighting'.

Farke (who no doubt appreciated Webber's public backing) is then interviewed soon after in the EDP, accepting that in some people's eyes, he's gone from a magician to a clown after the start of the season. "When you are praised so much in good times, it can be difficult to keep the feet grounded and then two weeks later, it could be the rotten tomatoes are being thrown. It's difficult. It is never easy."

"The criticism and spotlight are inevitable. It's never easy to deal with the situation or the pressure, but that's what you have to do if you want to work in this business. You always have to stay levelled, and in this business, things can change unbelievably quickly."

To ease the footballing pressure just for an afternoon, he could do worse than to pay a visit to the smallest traditional pub in the City – The Vine. Situated in a splendid location within the ever-popular Norwich Lanes, it's nestled just off the lively outdoor marketplace. Effervescent landlady Aey Allen doesn't let the size of the establishment deter her in any way though, as she gets the absolute most out of it that she can. Billed as 'small but perfectly formed', the Vine is also a 'go-to' destination for anyone looking for excellent Thai cuisine. It is also host to a variety of other well-supported activities that include winter and summer beer festivals, a weekly quiz night, weekly special offer nights for students and for CAMRA members, whilst also being a loyal and active participant of the annual Norwich City of Ale Festival. It's even available for hire each Sunday for that special occasion.

Remarkably, Aey had no experience in the trade before taking on the pub in 2008. After her marriage had broken down, she was faced with the stark choice of returning to Thailand or finding a challenge in Norwich and, although she remembers it being both stressful and scary, she picked the latter option. After disappointingly just missing out on obtaining the tenancy of the Woolpack (on Muspole Street), she found out that the Vine was available after a chance visit there one day, and this time her application was successful. She received the offer of help from several worried family members, but she rejected these as she was adamant she wanted to do this by herself.

Fast approaching 14 years at the helm, Aey prides herself on always trying her best, striving to provide a welcoming place for customers who she naturally sees as friends. She also believes that if people (particularly the locals) see that someone is making the effort, they are likely to appreciate this, and one particular patron who often finds his way here is none other than revered writer, journalist and real ale campaigner, Roger Protz.

Being included in the Good Beer Guide since 2011, Aey always keeps four local ales on tap, often selecting these after a request from trusted regulars (she also has a love of real ale herself and has another way of choosing what to have on – if she is an admirer of the product it is likely to be selected).

It is a measure of Aey's popularity and a definite sign of the respect she receives from the Norwich public if we take a look back to April 2021 when English hostelries were just coming out of yet another covid lockdown. Pubs were told by the government that they could open but only to serve customers if they were sat outside, thus causing an immediate issue for Aey, as she only has room on Dove Street for two tables. First of all, a neighbour assisted by offering the space up outside his premises, meaning that seven tables would now be available. A further problem was then encountered as a Norfolk Constabulary Traffic Management Officer raised fears over whether there was enough space for emergency vehicles to pass, and this is when the help really kicked in. A whole host of people contested the decision, including friends, customers, publicans, brewers, beer writers and newspapers and happily, the initial objection was removed, and an appreciative Aey was allowed to trade just a week later.

So, how much longer has Aey got left at the Vine? Well, it's good news as being a long-lease tenant, she has signed up for at least another seven years, and who knows after that? If she is still enjoying it, she could stay for even longer. There's no pressure from anyone here wanting her to depart any time sooner, unlike the under-fire Head Coach of a local football club, desperate for a victory in the next fixture.

The morning of the Leeds game did not feel like the beginning of a proper match day. Admittedly, I'm not a fan in any shape or form of unconventional kick-off times (moved solely to cater for the armchair fan) and unapologetically favour the traditional Saturday afternoon 3 o'clock fixtures. But even so, there was a definite early eeriness to the City as I made my way to the Glasshouse pub on Wensum Street for a much-needed breakfast. There was a dark foreboding sky advertising rain; a stiff, unfriendly, slightly chilly breeze disrupting and scattering the drunkenly discarded fast-food cartons and the empty, plastic cheap-cider bottles from the night before as I made my way along Colegate.

The delectable Denise had requested a lie-in, life and soul Paul was meeting an ex-Army colleague, dour and proud Yorkshireman Wiggy had remained in Salop for the weekend while Sheffield-based Richard was 'on his way' but suffering from the displeasure of being sat on a rail replacement bus from Peterborough. Meanwhile (and mercifully), the overly-proud Peacocks from West Yorkshire had yet to land. How did I know? Because it was still so quiet, and anyone familiar with Leeds fans will be more than aware that it is an impossibility for any of them to be discreet. If there are any in your vicinity, you can always hear one (always unnecessarily loudly) wittering away with "I'M FROM LEEDS ME I AM/WE'RE EUROPEAN CHAMPIONS WE ARE / WE TAKE MILLIONS EVERYWHERE WE GO WE DO /LEEDS LEEDS YORKSHIRE LEEDS LEEDS." A recent unofficial survey has indicated that if a Leeds fan was to bid you "GOOD MORNING LOVE" in Tombland, there is a very good chance that someone would overhear him up on the coast in Sea Palling.

The Glasshouse had a few customers but not half as many as I expected. Was there really going to be a very important Premier League fixture kicking off in less than five hours just down the road? A couple of nearby staff members killed time by discussing local house prices, and another asked me if there was a match on today and, if so, what time did it start – all strange.

My eagerly awaited full English arrived, courtesy of a slightly concerned-looking waitress. "Have you heard about the toast?" she earnestly inquired. I slowly started to shake my head, my brain not totally processing the question – had the toast done a runner, had it committed a crime, was it having an affair? – before she kindly came to my rescue, quickly adding, "Well, we don't have any."

I then made my way the short distance around to the trusty Wig & Pen, again not passing a soul on my walk. Happily, the loyal group of Norwich fans who use this pub as their base were already in situ, contentedly quaffing their pre-match beers, although unpromisingly, initial conversations indicated that not many of them were expecting a City victory. So much for Stuart Webber's rallying cry of not to give up on the team just yet…

The team news announced an hour before kick-off only appeared to strengthen this view. The continued inclusion of the young American striker Josh Sargent seemed to particularly provoke unanimous angst. Lamentably (and after only nine games where, let's not forget, not one of the players had covered themselves in any sort of glory) it would appear that he is on a fast track to becoming the latest scapegoat for some supporters, thus attracting the collective blame for his and his teammates shortcomings so far. At some stage, very soon, Josh would need to score a goal, Norwich would need to win a game in order to change the mood – they would need to 'show some teeth', as Webber desired.

Ultimately, the recovery was not to kick start this particular afternoon. At the final whistle, even as the earlier mentioned dark, foreboding clouds had been replaced with sunnier skies, it was still gloom and doom on the Carrow Road pitch as the visitors emerged triumphant with a 2-1 victory. First-half snapshots from Pukki and Normann both fizzed past a rooted-to-the-spot keeper, Meslier – they unfortunately also fizzed the wrong side of the post. The game was settled not long after halftime during a madcap, error-laden four minutes. Firstly, Raphina (56 mins) put Leeds in control, slotting home through Krul's legs after being aided by a couple of ricochets off last-ditch, diving challenges from Norwich defenders.

Then we had a genuine moment to savour. From the kickoff, Norwich went on the attack and immediately won a corner as Meslier nonchalantly side-footed the ball out as he tried to locate his full back. As the home crowd roared 'Come on you Yellows' more in hope than expectation Rashica darted the ball into a crowded box where it was met majestically by Andrew Omobamidele (58 mins), who thumped in a header that gloriously flew into the net off the underside of the crossbar to bring the scores level. A fantastic moment for the young Irishman (his first senior goal) sparking unbridled joy amongst the delirious home faithful – the first goal scored by their team since Pukki levelled against Watford over a month ago on the 18th of September.

I was just in the process of re-acquainting my posterior with my WALL seat after joyously celebrating the equaliser when Leeds retaliated with an attack of their own. Initially, a probing forward pass was intercepted by Ozan Kabak, who instantly and needlessly gave the ball away. Within a split second Rodrigo (60 mins) belted a left-footer goal-wards that dipped inexcusably under a diving Krul. Two big errors in five seconds, and Norwich were once again behind, and other than a couple of half-chances for McLean and Placheta never looked like getting anything out of the game. They left the field to a crescendo of boos as many of the home crowd vented their displeasure at the result.

As the Bees of Brentford come buzzing into view for next Saturday's game at their shiny new hive, there were definitely several unanswered questions that were perplexing Norwich fans. For example:

How can a team that had won the Championship after a record-breaking season be failing so badly?

How can the performances of the promising new signings made by City – in transfers dealings classed by Jurgen Klopp as being 'sensational' – be so underwhelming?

Two and a half months and ten games into the season, why were we still waiting for the team 'to gel'?

Why are we yet to experience any of the 'beautiful moments' that Daniel Farke had been so confident that we could expect?

Why was the 'defending behaviour' yet to consistently improve?

Could the prospective confidence issues that concerned Chris Sutton earlier in the season have come to the fore?

Whatever the answers may be to the above queries, Norwich (and Farke in particular) will be more than frantic not to add any more to 'stats don't lie' Benjamin's compilation of damning data. Regrettably, and at this still relatively early stage of the season, it looks like Psychic Sandra has already lost her birthday money.

CHAPTER 6

SOUTHAMPTON (H)

20TH NOVEMBER 2021

As Norwich City were heading to West London, bottom of the pile with two points from 10 games, Daniel Farke was fielding questions on his own future at the pre-match press conference.

"Let's be honest, if our bus driver had been in charge for the past ten games, he could not be there with any less points. He is a great guy, but I don't think he would like to do my job at the minute."

"But there is also no guarantee if someone else was in charge, maybe one of the top coaches like Jurgen Klopp or Thomas Tuchel or Pep Guardiola, they would have won more points."

"On this level, it is not what happens in the past but who is the right guy in charge to lead this club and develop these players. Whether that was last season or these last ten games."

Bullishly, he insisted he would 'walk' if he felt he was not the right coach to get City firing.

The only question I was fielding as my train entered Kew Bridge station early on the Saturday morning was what local hostelries I was going to frequent. In an area (including Brentford and Chiswick) awash with decent pubs, I decided on the Royal Horse Guardsman (a small, comfortable, single bar, street corner local), the Black Dog Beer House (7 cask ales available, busy with football and rugby union fans) and the beguilingly named One over the Ait (a cavernous Fullers brewery pub that features a boat precariously hanging directly above the bar).

But what's an 'Ait' Neil, I hear you ask? Well, thanks for inquiring. In this case, it's a long 4,572-acre uninhabited island in the River Thames with the river flowing directly alongside the pub. People had actually lived there back in the eighteenth century, the main building being a notorious establishment called the Three Swans. Situated on the Brentford bank opposite the east end of Watermans Park, it was closed in 1796 after complaints from Kew Green locals who were continually annoyed at the rowdy and often immoral behaviour of the patrons. One resident, Robert Hunter, wrote at the time, 'Brentford Ait is a great nuisance to this parish and the neighbourhoods on both sides of the river. The house of entertainment has long been a harbour of the men and women of the worst description, where riotous and indecent scenes are often exhibited' – over 200 years later, he could quite unerringly be describing Norwich's Prince of Wales Road on any given Saturday evening.

Other than the beers on offer, I also wanted to visit the 'One over the Ait' as it was situated in the very location where Brentford FC had been formed in October 1889.

Originally a boathouse for the local rowing club, the members voted that a new association football club was to be formed and that they would wear salmon, claret and light blue colours. They were obviously keen on avoiding any problematic colour clashes.

I sat outside on the pub's side terrace with my two pints of Fullers London Pride (wisely bulk buying as the pub was rammed), contentedly overlooking the Thames. I was beginning to have a really good feeling about the upcoming fixture for a few reasons. I'd just found out that the U18s had won for the first time this season, beating Birmingham City 3-1 (with Kenny Coker coming on as a late substitute). The initial positive seed, however, had been sown the previous evening. Remember the pub landlord from the previous chapter who felt a need to knock people's heads off? Well, I had a chance meeting with him, and he was adamant that Norwich would be victorious. "Mate, get your money on Norwich to win 2-1 tomorrow. I've had a tenner on them - easy money. Brentford have lost their last three and are there for the taking." He has no affiliation to Norwich as he's a Spurs fan – a random statement that certainly got me thinking.

Later on the same evening, the U23's score came in from Carrow Road – they'd beaten Nottingham Forest 4-2, a further positive sign.

So, with two wins for the Academy teams plus City being randomly (and yet confidently) tipped, could I really start to believe? Could we really be on the cusp of our first league win of the season? Would this be the first of the 'beautiful moments' Farke had promised us?

The Brentford Community Stadium is wedged rather

cleverly into a Wye. But what's a 'Wye' Neil, I hear you ask? Well, thanks for inquiring. In this case, it's a triangular joining arrangement of three rail lines with a railroad switch at each corner connecting to each incoming line. It's incredible that a fit-for-purpose Premier League ground has been built within such space limitations, and yet the unique design is certainly distinctive, far and away from the usual identikit bowl-like stadiums that we are all used to seeing being built, particularly during the last twenty years.

From the moment the referee blew his whistle to start the game, things seemed different. Passion, desire, beautiful football (or should that be Farkeball), last-ditch trojan-like defending, togetherness with Normann and Gibson in particular, constantly cajoling teammates, and GOALS x 2! The fans sang loudly and proudly throughout the 90 minutes, with the oft-repeated "Daniel Farke's Yellow Army" seeming to fit the atmosphere very well.

City made a dream start after 6 minutes when Mathias Normann slotted in from the edge of the area after a good run, obviously helping the vocal output from the visitor's section containing 1,700 Canaries – the first goal scored by Norwich away from Carrow Road this season. Pukki then despatched a penalty in the 29th minute to make it 2-0, his 70th goal for the club in 138 games moving him to eighth among the club's all-time top goalscorers, tied with John Deehan. Brentford did pull a goal back in the second half, but City held on for a much-needed memorable first league win, momentarily moving them off the foot of the table.

At full time the jubilant players came over to jointly celebrate with the fans, backed up by their boss, the proud

Head Coach, who treated us to his customary four 'olé victory waves'. All was very well with the world.

It's not very often that we hear from Teemu Pukki (he seemingly is a man of few words who very rarely does club interviews), but after the game, speaking to the EDP, he said, "I think we need to forget those first ten games and start from here. There are 27 league games left, and now it starts for us. We've got the first win and we need to start getting more results like this. There were a lot of happy faces in the locker room, and it's good to go from here now." Nothing remarkable in his initial musings then, all very standard after-match football comments so far.

He was then asked to give his views on the performance of goalscorer Normann and it's here where the interview became interesting and, for me, pertinent to the results experienced to date. "A great goal from him and also the assist was pretty good, so I think that's a good sign that our new players are starting to show up – and also all of us, we all need to step up. We haven't been good enough either, so we need to be better if we want to compete at this level." – could this be interpreted from our Finnish striker that he now believed that new and old teammates were finally and mercifully beginning 'to gel'?

I made my way back to the 'One over the Ait', where I was greeted by one of the doormen. "Welcome back, Sir. Good to see you again. I hope you've had a good afternoon." Well, wasn't that a lovely, friendly reception, I thought...but did he really recognise me from earlier; as I've already mentioned, the pub was rammed. I cheekily enquired, "OK, I'm going to test you now, just to see how good you really are at your job. Where was I sat beforehand?"

With a big triumphant smile on his face, he immediately pointed over to the exact spot on the side terrace, saying, "You were seated over there, Sir, of course, contentedly overlooking the Thames." I shook his hand in awe.

The celebratory beers continued to flow in Kew Bridge before I made my way back to the King's Cross/St Pancras conurbation, popping into the Parcel Yard pub, yet another vast building operated by Fullers brewery. I was rather enjoying a pint of their Extra Special Bitter (a twice-named world champion beer), albeit slightly bemused by the antics of a group of England rugby union fans who were all of a certain age. They had obviously given the egg-shaped ball 'a good kicking' and were now going through their repertoire of bawdy ballads, eagerly encouraged by an exuberant associate who was bashing away on an empty (and now decorative) wooden cask with all the commitment and enthusiasm of a man who truly believed he was one of the percussionists in an Adam & The Ants tribute band. Then my phone rang. It was my eldest daughter Paige.

"Dad. He's been sacked!" I queried who she was talking about. "Farke – he's gone with immediate effect." Whether it was the beer I'd drunk, the beer the rugby fans had drunk and the general bedlam in the pub but it was very difficult to process the message. How could he have been sacked after such a victory? It must have been a pre-meditated move by the club. The decision must have been made earlier that, whatever the result at the Brentford Community Stadium, he had to go.

A sombre, disorientating train journey followed on the

way back to Chesterfield, the euphoria of the first win of the season being severely tempered by the announcement that we were now on the hunt for a new Head Coach. It was a definite step away from the familiar and an uncomfortable lunge into the unknown. The latest betting odds on prospective appointments the following morning only compounded this feeling – Sam Allardyce, Garry Monk and John Terry being amongst the usual depressing suspects promoted by betting companies and the media whenever a club is on the lookout for a new manager.

The press and social media were overflowing with comments relating to the sacking and tributes from players.

First of all, we heard from the man responsible for pulling the trigger, Sporting Director Stuart Webber, in an official club statement "In continuing to demand the very best for our football club, this decision was not an easy one. I know how determined Daniel and his staff were to succeed at this level, but we feel that now is the right time for a change to give ourselves the best opportunity of retaining our Premier League status. All at Norwich City should be forever grateful to Daniel and his staff for the significant role they have played in our journey. They helped deliver two Championship titles, many memorable moments and they all fully bought into our philosophy and what it means to be part of this football club. Daniel and his staff will always be welcome back here. I'd like to take this opportunity to thank them all for their hard work and wish them well for the future."

Next came the acknowledgements from the players, mainly on Instagram and Twitter. Here's a selection:

- **Max Aarons** - "Boss, thank you for helping me realise my dream. Through everything, you have given me this opportunity and been there for me no matter what. Good luck in everything you do in the future. Thank you for everything Boss."
- **Angus Gunn** – "What this man has done for myself, this club & the city is incredible. Thank you for everything Boss."
- **Ben Gibson** – "Boss – you believed in me when it seemed like nobody else did. The memories will never be forgotten, thank you."
- **Adam Idah** – "I wish you all the best with your next chapter boss. Made a little boys dreams come true. Thank you for everything and good luck."
- **Tim Krul** – "Boss, thank you for helping me realise my dream. Through everything, you have given me this opportunity and been there for me no matter what. Good luck in everything you do in the future. Thank you for everything Boss."

Finally, we heard from the man himself less than 24 hours after his reign came to an abrupt end. In a typically classy message to the fans, via The Athletic website, he said: "We, and by that I mean our coaching staff of Edmund Riemer, Christopher John, Chris Domogalla and myself, have had a great time at Norwich City, which has now come to an end. We leave Norwich with great pride. Having worked for this exceptional club for almost four and a half years means a lot to us. Our special thanks go to the fans who have always supported the team and us, making the many great moments at Carrow Road unforgettable. Two promotions to the Premier League together will connect us forever. Football is a short-term business, and for that, we were quite long-term in Norwich because it was made possible by Delia Smith, Michael Wynn Jones and Stuart Webber. Goodbye, Canaries. We'll see you again."

And with that, he had gone. We would no longer bear witness to his attacking yet patient style of football, his idiosyncratic exuberance, the passionate monologues and selection bravery. We would no longer be hearing of players who needed to have fire in their bellies and ice in their heads, of dancing on the tables after a victory, of facing the rotten tomatoes after a defeat, of his team being greedy for the three points.

To be Head Coach of Norwich City Football Club genuinely seemed to mean the world to him, and for that, there will always be a place in my yellow and green heart for the unknown German who came to manage my club and gave us all a belief, not to mention some of the most memorable footballing days ever. The new boss had better be good. We know it's not going to be the bus driver; we know it's not going to be Klopp, Tuchel or Guardiola but what we do know is the new man has some pretty big and impressive shoes to fill.

There then followed, yet another international break. I usually detest these with a passion, although Teemu Pukki would no doubt be viewing the situation contrarily as he looked to make his 100th appearance for Finland (which he successively achieved against France, becoming only the 5th person to accomplish this milestone for the 'Huuhkajat' – or the 'Eagle-Owls' to you and I). This latest disruption to the domestic football calendar was going to be different to the norm though, with the hunt for a new gaffer already in progress.

The media frenzy went into full swing immediately, with the initial smart money being on ex-Chelsea and England star Frank Lampard, although the impressive coach of Norwegian team FK Bodø/Glimt, Kjetil Knutsen, was also getting a mention and seemed to be a more suitable option. Norwich City expectedly and typically remained as taciturn as the tightest-lipped clam.

There was then a rather interesting development over in Birmingham where Aston Villa announced that they too had terminated the contract of their Head Coach, Dean Smith, after five defeats on the spin. His time there was generally considered to have been a success, with promotion gained to the Premier League in 2019 before subsequently consolidating the club in the top tier. He'd also taken them to the 2019/2020 League Cup Final but what was probably as notable (to any attentive Norwich eyes and ears) was that he had played a key role in the development of precocious talent Jack Grealish before his £100m move to Manchester City.

Talksport (via an exclusive from Adam Goodwin) then spectacularly jumped the gun by announcing that Lampard had got the job, citing good work in developing young players during his spell in charge at Derby County, such as the on-loan Chelsea pair Mason Mount and Fikayo Tomori. Fascinatingly the article finished with a link to Aston Villa mentioning that Steven Gerrard had been appointed as their new boss and that it would be the first time that he and Lampard would manage a club in the same division at the same time. The footnote advertised 'Villa face Norwich on December 14 at Carrow Road'. Little did they (Talksport) know at the time the actual and ensuing significance relevant to this particular fixture.

It was to be a further four days before an official declaration was made on the new incumbent, and it wasn't to be Lampard or Knutsen (or even someone else who was totally unknown or hadn't been mentioned, which is what some supporters believed could have happened). Norwich City announced Dean Smith as their new main man, and he would be joined at the club by his assistant Craig Shakespeare. Here's what Stuart Webber had to say:

"We are delighted to have appointed Dean as our new head coach. I have admired his work for some time, and he has been a long-term target in the event that we needed to appoint a new head coach."

"He shares the same values and vision as the club, has a proven track record of winning games in the Premier League as well as developing players and building a winning culture and mentality." Smith had agreed a two and a half year contract.

It was hoped this was a fresh start for everyone, a clean slate particularly for the players with new voices, new people and changes to training sessions, hopefully stimulating an immediate recovery and, ultimately, Premier League survival.

In Smith's first official press conference, he pointedly made several references to there being 27 games remaining in which to save Norwich's season. There was no chest-thumping, no over-the-top proclamations and no promises. He talked a lot of common sense, revealing a grounded individual who believed that he had the squad necessary to do the job – he now required them to believe they could succeed. Human touches were evident too, with references to his family (very important to him) and, when asked how he had filled his time while 'between jobs', he confessed, with a smile on his face, "I have a bit of OCD in me... I check the fridge to see if the ham is out of date and things like that." Finally, there was a tasteful reference to his predecessor when he said, "I am also very respectful of the job he has done, and these are big boots to fill."

Football can be a funny old game at times, can't it? Dean Smith's last game in charge for Aston Villa was a 1-0 loss away to Southampton, and his first game in charge of Norwich? Of course, it's a home game against the Saints - what a chance for immediate revenge.

I was reminded of his OCD reference on the Saturday morning, as I made my way east for the game courtesy of East Midlands Railways. Several Nottingham Forest fans (on their way to Reading) entered my carriage at the stations of Alfreton, Langley Mill and Ilkeston. They all appeared to know each other and were in their late teens/early twenties. As the last of them got on at the latter station, small-talk soon lurched alarmingly to this mental health condition.

"How long did it take you to get out of the house this morning then?"

"Fuckin 'ell, ages mate, Thought I was never gunna get away."

"What do you have to do?"

"Well, at the moment, I have to finish off by locking the door, then trying the handle four times. Then I walk away, then turn back, then try the handle another four times. Then I keep doing that another twice until I can walk down the drive. Luckily this morning, I didn't have to turn round anymore, although I nearly did a few times."

There was an equal mix of reaction to this, with half of his friends sniggering while the others genuinely looked rightly concerned. One of these then volunteered his own personal routine "I have to lock the door then try the handle four times as well. Then I have to kick the door, walk down the path, then kick the dustbin. Only when I've kicked the dustbin do I know that the door is really locked."

As we neared the approach to Nottingham station, we got to hear from the final Forest contributor. "I've had issues this morning as well. Had to go back in the house twice to make sure I'd turned my fucking straighteners off." There was general hilarity to this proclamation – his hair was two inches long, maximum.

After leaving the train, today's main pre-match port of call is the Trafford Arms on Grove Road, a mere 10-minute walk from the top end of the busy shopping thoroughfare of St Stephens Street. I'm in the company of life and soul Paul (who not surprisingly has already predicted a 4-0 home win) and there, waiting to greet us behind the bar, is Simon Davey, who's a very safe pair of hands to call upon particularly within the pub environs of Norwich and North Suffolk. After vast experience gained in a number of roles at (amongst others) Potters Kiln & Triangle Tavern in Lowestoft and Duke of Wellington, Ribs of Beef and the Glasshouse in the City, it is the Trafford where he is now to be found champing at the bit as Assistant Manager.

As further knowledge has also been acquired in the East

Midlands cities of Derby (at The Brunswick – both behind the bar and in the adjacent brewery) and Nottingham (at The Fox & Crown, Old Basford), I compare his varied journey so far with that of another safe pair of hands - those of Norwich City goalkeeper Michael McGovern. Similar to Simon, McGovern has intermittently switched between the odd elevated spell as the Number One at most of his eight professional clubs (including St Johnstone, Ross County, Falkirk and Hamilton Academicals) to that of the more frequent dependable deputy, with ex-boss Daniel Farke often publicly declaring his total trust in the Northern Irishman.

It's not just the dependability that the Trafford Arms benefits from though, as Simon has obtained a wealth of experience and expertise within the arena of real ale, cementing the pub's reputation as one of Norwich's flagship alehouses. Situated on the junction of Grove Road and Trafford Road, there are plenty of chimney pots surrounding the pub in this vibrant suburb. On a match day, it's usually bustling with thirsty Norwich fans that still have to pass the added temptations of Kings Arms, Freemasons and the Rose on their way to the match – it's approximately a 25-minute walk away from the ground.

The interior is mainly open plan and yet comfortable with plenty of bare, red brick features after a major refurb in 1982. Interestingly, this is actually the second Trafford Arms on this site (the third if you include the infamous 'Chicken House'). The original, built in the 1880s, was an attractive three-storey building that was enhanced in appearance by a Dutch Gable effect frontage (similar to, although much larger than, the look of the Adam & Eve on Bishopgate).

This building was severely damaged through enemy bombing in 1942. With quick thinking and a spot of creativity by landlord Nobby Clarke and the pub was re-opened in a temporary wooden building, converted from the palatial residence housing a large number of broilers – hence the new name of the 'Chicken House' - and this was still in use until the first half of the present building was finally completed in the Autumn of 1955. It was a while later that the second half was added, and this is what we now associate with being the lounge area.

Simon has aspirations that the Trafford becomes the top real ale pub in Norwich, no mean feat in a place where several other establishments are also striving for the same accolade (and two days after my visit, the pub proudly announced its inclusion in the prestigious 2022 Good Beer Guide). However, it is these types of hard-earned awards that mean the most – again, similar to how Michael McGovern achieved his Player of the Season awards while at Falkirk.

A couple of hours later, and it was time to make our way to the stadium, negotiating the sheer precipice of the path down to King Street from Southgate Lane, today made more of a challenge by way of a carpet of damp and skiddy fallen autumn leaves. It's also fair to report that the leg joints take a battering on this route as well, and you can almost hear the collective creaking and cracking of complaining knees.

On the stroke of kick-off, Dean Smith took to the turf to introduce himself to the supporters of his new team and was instantaneously welcomed with an enthusiastic cry of "Deano! Deano!" He may only have been at the club for less than a week, but there already appeared to be something about his character that had immediately endeared him to us in this corner of East Anglia. The king is dead; long live the king.

It wasn't an ideal start for the Canaries. There was an all too painfully familiar ring to it as a combination of defensive weakness, and bad luck ended in the visitors going in front in the 4th minute. We've been here before, of course, the majority of the crowd falling silent (many with head in hands) while a section of the South Stand celebrate joyously.

What happened next was a rather pleasant surprise. Three minutes later, Milot Rashica scruffily bundled over Southampton speedster Walker-Peters but was waved on by the referee, Martin Atkinson (who went on to have an excellent game). The Kosovan winger exchanged passes with Max Aarons, before finally releasing the full-back to the by-line. Aarons was off-balance as he dug out a cross, but the delivery was spot on, and talisman Pukki darted in to divert a header powerfully inside the near post.

This was as good as it got for the home team during the first 45 minutes as they were dispiritingly second best to a visiting team that had them relentlessly penned back, probing effectively down both flanks time and again. Still, when the halftime whistle was blown, the scores were still level as Southampton failed to be both ruthless and clinical in their attempts to put the game to bed. Could the new head coach now have a positive impact and manage to get his team to turn the tide?

First of all, he hooked the lacklustre and ineffective Todd Cantwell and replaced him with the more energetic Josh

Sargent, swapping Rashica over to his favoured left flank. He also implored his team to get a toe-hold in the game by 'pushing up higher'. Slowly but surely, they began to grow into the match and then continued to have the better of the second half, although, much like Southampton earlier, failing to create too many clear opportunities. Mathias Normann saw a long-range effort go just over in the 66th minute, and then an inspired Pukki forced a fine reaction save from Alex McCarthy moments later.

With 11 minutes remaining, the decisive moment arrived. A long spell of Norwich possession ended with a Rashica cross being diverted over the bar. Billy Gilmour stepped up for the corner, drifted it to the back post and there was the skipper Grant Hanley, on his 30th birthday, bouncing a downwards header over the outstretched arm of the goalie and into the roof of the net. Ladies and gentlemen, boys and girls, we have lift-off at Carrow Road!

Norwich survived late pressure and specifically a late alarm when Theo Walcott nearly equalised with a free header, thus leaving Carrow Road to spontaneously erupt in joyousness and overall relief at the 2-1 victory. As pumped-up keeper Krul left the pitch, it seemed rather fitting that the first person to greet and then congratulate him on his performance was the trusty Michael McGovern.

Southampton and England midfielder James Ward-Prowse reflected afterwards in the Southern Daily Echo, "We just stopped doing what we were doing in the first half. We stopped being brave on the ball, stopped creating the chances."

"We just got outperformed a little bit. We could feel the emotion in the stands, energy in the stands with the new manager (Dean Smith) and the supporters were all backing him."

"We did well in the first half, but they kind of overpowered us, and the fans definitely played a big part in spurring their team on."

As I rushed down Koblenz Avenue on my way to Thorpe Station, 'Dean Smith's yellow army' rang out into the chilly, early evening Norfolk air. The result had ultimately seen Norwich lift themselves off the bottom of the table with two wins in two, their new era getting off to a perfect start.

CHAPTER 7

WOLVERHAMPTON WANDERERS (H)

27TH NOVEMBER 2021

F ollowing the heartening victory over the Saints, Norwich could (and most probably should) have acquired another 3 points against the high-flying Wanderers. An inability to take at least 1 of 4 presentable chances meant that they had to settle for a point in a 0-0 draw. On another day, Pukki could have added a brace to his already burgeoning total, while Max Aarons and Lukas Rupp could have been uncorking a bottle of the fizzy stuff while celebrating their first Premier League goals.

Two other major plusses had been the performances of Billy Gilmour and Milot Rashica, surely their best respective games of the season so far. Both of them have a natural instinct to get involved and attack with the ball at their feet, but perhaps as important was that they had demonstrated a tenacious desire to provide the defensive ballast that is often overlooked. It had definitely been a battling performance by the home team in general that saw the visitors pinned to the ropes for large periods of the second half; they would certainly board the bus back to Molineux knowing that they had been in a game.

Of course, there had been the usual early display of calamitous defending as skipper Hanley put his goalkeeper in trouble with a suicidal back pass. For once, the opposition refused to scrutinise the dental structure of this particular green and yellow festooned stallion, with a sprawling Krul saving the resultant shot with his legs then thankfully watching the ball bounce off to relative safety.

There was very little else for the Dutch international to deal with for the remainder of the game other than back-passes (as a means of retaining and rotating possession) plus routine catches from misplaced crosses. It was clear that Norwich's defensive work across the whole pitch had drastically improved, particularly since the debacle at Stamford Bridge in October. Chances were also being created after upgraded approach work, but they would now need to start taking more of them…

In the week leading up to the Wolverhampton game, there had been three major announcements regarding Norwich City. Firstly, we were informed there was to be a new official badge that was to be used across all club branding from June 2022. This was the first alteration for 50 years to the much-loved emblem, easily identifiable and consisting of:

1. An off-centre, rather large canary (in comparison to the ball it is stood on) with somewhat dodgy lop-sided tail feathers and an unnervingly gazing eye. I'm convinced it's winked at me on a few occasions in the past, although admittedly, this has usually been when I'm on the train home from a game, and I've been on my last can of beer.

2. A rudimentary-looking castle consisting of a door, 2 windows and 5 turrets (when we all know that there are actually 9 turrets on each side of Norwich Castle, don't we?)

3. A quite magnificent heraldic lion, sporting two triangular eyes, a triangular mouth and an outrageously long and elaborate tail (hurrah for the lion!). I personally think it's been wonderful that this little chappie has been cheerfully waving to us all with his right paw for the last half-century.

The club explained it's "a modernised, evolved crest which will ensure consistency across all digital, print and physical branding."

"The new crest features a redesigned lion, castle and canary, each of which has been redrawn to overcome the technical issues found. By simplifying the elements and removing a lot of the unnecessary detail, the crest now renders strongly both small and large scale."

When comparing the old and new badges side by side, they are actually very similar with (as the club acknowledges) much of the detail eliminated in the new one. However, viewing the newer version in isolation is akin to ordering a pint of alcoholic beverage and unknowingly being given the 0% version or ordering an espresso and receiving decaf. I'm sure we'll get used to it though, in time.

Not everyone was in favour of the new design, and I'll leave the last word on the crest (and principally concerning the lion) to the former chairman of the Heraldry Society, Steve Ashley, who (revealing his most inner Craig Revel Horwood), in a letter to the Norwich Evening News complained "The feeble lion on the proposed new badge is neither heraldic nor realistic. Its head fails to threaten, it has weak paws and claws, and its rather awkward rear legs lack movement, being closer in appearance to those of a kangaroo."

The second key announcement of the week concerning Norwich City (again via the official website canaries.co.uk) was that Sporting Director Stuart Webber had agreed a new 12-month rolling contract that would commence at the completion of the current season. This type of agreement does provide a certain amount of stability, although it is definitely more flexible than a fixed-term one; as Webber explained, "The trust I have with Delia and Michael is that if the day comes when they want me to leave the next second, then not a problem, and likewise if the time comes when I want to have some time out."

The third announcement relating to the club, and in what can only be described as a bombshell, was regarding life and soul Paul, who, seemingly overnight, had morphed into disgruntled and disillusioned Paul. In a text sent to me towards the end of the week, he confessed to currently being fed up with football (particularly the Premier League) and had decided to take some time out, not only missing the upcoming Wolves fixture but also the next scheduled home game against Manchester United. Considering that this comes after back-to-back victories is not only a major surprise but also a little suspicious. Is there more to this than meets the eye? I shall have to go full-on Sherlock Holmes, don my Inverness cape and deerstalker and commence investigation…

So, with Paul not in attendance pre-match, I decided to pay a visit to Norwich Crematorium Gardens to pay my respects at the memorial to recently departed and bloody good mate and drinking buddy, Nige. Afterwards, as I was walking back into the City, I chose to call into the Mitre.

OK, I know you're thinking, 'but this is not a traditional pub anymore' and this is, of course, correct. However, I think it's well worth telling the story of this Tudor-revival-style building that is a mere 10-minute walk along the Earlham Road from the Roman Catholic cathedral.

To sufficiently appreciate the construction, it helps if you happen to be a fully paid-up member of the Symmetrophile Society, which I am very close to being. For example, I've always forbidden myself from having a tattoo as I'm pretty damned sure that I would have to have the adorned limb removed if the permanent image appeared to be slightly skew-whiff. There are no such issues here though, as the Mitre is a perfect proportionately-balanced delight, with a jettied, central section flanked by timbered side bays featuring attractive herringbone brick infills.

Continuing the theme of symmetry, a snapshot taken in 1933 by prolific Norfolk photographer George Plunkett comfortingly shows lanterns fixed above left, central and right doors. It is pleasing to see the current owners and next-door neighbours, St. Thomas Church Norwich (STN), are also following the same idyll with strategically placed yellow security alarms placed on either side of upstairs windows.

Plunkett's photo, seemingly taken on a sunny day, shows a pub that looks potentially dark and foreboding on the inside. Indeed, selected customer comments logged on the 'Beer in the Evening' website dating from 2005–2009 include (copied word for word, their spelling and grammar – not mine) the following:

"Not a bad gaff, beer is ok, prices as good as anywhere, clientele, seem for the main part, ok. Main whing is it's too dark, atmosphere is fine but it's like drinking in a coal shed. I know electric isn't cheap but c'mom now, nice to be able to see what your drinking."

"Chav Central, nuff said."

"The worst pub in the golden triangle, its only saving grace is that it's quite cheap for the area."

It's perhaps not too surprising then, that the pub suffered a change of use to a Chinese takeaway shortly afterwards in 2011, but even this reincarnation was for a relatively short-lived four years.

It wasn't that the Mitre was always short of notable patrons though. Apparently, the Right Honourable Sir Norman Lamb (ex-Liberal Democrat MP for North Norfolk and long-standing Canaries fan) was present in the pub when Jeremy Goss rifled home THAT volley in the Munich

Olympic Stadium on the glorious evening of 19 October 1993 when City famously beat Bayern 2-1. This is one of those moments in life when any Norwich supporter of a certain vintage can relate back to 'where I was when Gossy scored'. For my part, I am pleased to report that I was dutifully taking my place in my one and only identity parade at Chesterfield Police Station, not as the main suspect, I may add.

Earlier that day, an urgent appeal had gone out around my workplace from the local police department for eight suitable males to take part in a line-up. Since I had been wisely prohibited from travelling to the game in Germany by my heavily pregnant wife, the delectable Denise (in fact, eldest daughter Paige was born less than 48 hours later), I happened to be available. We would be paid £10 each for our time and troubles; not a bad little earner for what we were informed would be a 30 minutes exercise, thereby giving me plenty of time to be home for kick-off.

All was well as eight professional, well-behaved and extremely mature adults entered the parade room and took seats in front of the one-way mirror. That was until a young constable entered with a box of black, cosmetic pens in order to draw a moustache on each of us to make us look more like the suspect. As the very basic and badly drawn whiskers started taking shape, it was apparent that the eight professional, well-behaved and extremely mature adults were transforming into naughty juveniles. Although, it is true that attempts were being made at this stage to stifle the sniggers, snorts and titters that were starting to become noticeable.

I can report that these minor neighs and whinnies soon

advanced into chuckles and chortles as one of my colleagues decided he had obtained more than a passing resemblance to Officer Crabtree from 'Allo Allo' uttering "Good moaning…..I have been disgeesed as a sispoct."

The chuckles and chortles then finally transformed into fully blown guffaws and chesty howls (with a random, singular, excitable parp) as, accompanied by his bemused Brief, the actual suspect entered the room looking remarkably like Officer Crabtree.

Despite repeated attempts by the harassed Chesterfield constable to calm the hysterical, 'Allo Allo' quoting shambles that was now being confused as a police line-up, there was not a chance that the parade could now take place. Worst of all, we had overrun, and I knew that I would miss the kick-off in Munich's Olympiastadion. We were all dismissed from our duties, shuffling out of the room like mischievous schoolchildren, scolded after a badly performed prank, never to be invited again. We didn't even get the tenner.

The Mitre, last listed as a public house in 2011, has been resurrected in recent times into a community café, bar and bistro after being purchased in 2015. A selection of Moon Gazer beers from the Norfolk Brewhouse in Hindringham are usually available in bottled format.

There are no darkness issues now as a two-year renovation (re-opening was 2017) has resulted in a light, airy, very modern interior. Also, thankfully, the splendid stained glass mitre images have been retained in the front windows flanking the main entrance.

On my early morning visit, for some unknown reason, I was craving poached eggs on toast for breakfast. "Good morning", greeted the young, friendly-looking waitress. "What are you fancying?"

"I'm really fancying poached eggs on toast, with a coffee, please," a reasonable request, I thought. I was, after all, in a café at breakfast time.

Anguished looks appeared on the faces of the waitress and the equally young waiter who had now joined her. "I'm not sure we can do that. We only have eggs for one local lady who usually comes in a couple of times a week. I'm going to have to ask the chef if it's possible, but I don't think she'll do it."

After a serious discussion and some stern, exasperated looks in my direction from the chef, the girl came back down the stairs from the kitchen to gladly inform me that "OK, on this one occasion she'll do it for you" with the lad adding "but please don't make a habit of ordering this and please, please don't tell anybody she's done it for you or else all hell with break loose!"

I sat down at my table, double-checking my surroundings. A strange, unworldly feeling came over me. Had I gone into the local DIY store or maybe a branch of a bank by mistake?

The lad reappeared. "By the way, we don't do normal sliced bread toast, you know. It'll have to be toasted ciabatta if that's alright with you?"

Half an hour passed (I even ordered another coffee) before the waiter triumphantly appeared with my prized breakfast. Call me perceptive, but I guessed there had been issues. "Sorry for the long wait, but the first couple of attempts with the poached eggs weren't very successful as we don't have the right type of vinegar."

I am delighted to report that the ad-hoc meal was absolutely delicious as well as being reasonably priced, even though it had to go "through the till as a bacon bap".

On my exit, I thoroughly thanked the staff for being so accommodating. I will be back at some stage for another breakfast offering, just probably not poached eggs on toast.

CHAPTER 8

MANCHESTER UNITED (H)

11TH DECEMBER 2021

Back in the heady days of September 1993, as Norwich City prepared to embark on their first (and so far only) European adventure, I remember being fascinated to find out that it was exactly the same distance of 201 miles, as the crow flies, between Norwich and Dutch city, Arnhem (home of UEFA Cup first-round opponents Vitesse) and Norwich and Newcastle (home of more familiar domestic adversaries).

It would perhaps be classed as an understatement to say it's a fair old trek by road from Carrow Road, Norwich, to St James Park, Newcastle. The quickest route is just over 250 miles and can be achieved in a mere five and a half hours if all goes to plan...that means no hold-ups, no road works, no accidents and no blumming tractors, caravans or extremely slow-moving lorries trundling along the A47 and A17. During daytime hours the trip can also be completed in roughly the same amount of time if public transport is your preferred option, although it would be advisable to factor in at least another hour as part of the journey would need to be taken with an East Midlands Railways train and this as we all know, could be cancelled or at best, delayed. It's at least a 10-hour round voyage, whichever way you look at it, with Norwich fans travelling back home after this particular Tuesday evening fixture unlikely to hit the sheets until after 3 a.m.

Imagine my amazement the morning after the game when I spotted the following headline accompanying Tristan Barclay's match report in The Sun: '*Canaries snatch late equaliser in relegation derby*'. A derby??? Traditionally this has always been a match played with fierce partisanship between local rivals from the same part of the country (i.e. Norwich City v Ipswich Town) or from the same city or town (i.e. Sheffield United v Sheffield Wednesday). These are games that are very special indeed, relished by fans and players alike. Surely a more appropriate description for the previous evening's game would be relegation 'battle', relegation 'scrap' or even relegation 'six-pointer'?

Whatever your preferred choice of noun, it has to be agreed that the match was certainly enthralling, especially after home defender, Ciaran Clark, was dismissed after just nine minutes for clumsily hauling back the marauding Pukki, the Finn intent on capitalising on a mistake by the defender. The expected onslaught from the Canaries never managed to materialise as the further back Newcastle's defensive position became entrenched Norwich's forward play was becoming as passive in equal measures; the arrows they were trying to fire were just paper darts, leaving the home team unscathed. At stages, it also appeared that they were hoping for things to happen rather than proactively making them happen. Newcastle, meanwhile, were strategically waiting for misplaced passes, alert to catching the visitors on the break, aided by the lightning-quick French winger, Allan Saint-Maximin.

Now, some eagle-eyed opinionated observers of this Norwich vintage will have a comprehensive list of suggestions where improvements could be made (e.g. cut out defensive errors, move the ball quicker, be more clinical in attack), all of which can be worked upon in training by dedicated coaches. However, there is one very important aspect of 'game management' where they definitely need to become better and wiser in order to gain an advantage, and that is in the 'dark arts' practice of appealing. Let me try and explain…

There were two very similar instances that happened either side of half-time, one for each team, where the respective players' immediate responses varied substantially from the initial decisions made by the referee. Firstly, City's Christos Tzolis had a goal-bound header parried by the arm (outstretched to the side of his body) of Newcastle defender Fabian Schär, who then, for some inexplicable reason, immediately started to limp like he'd sprained his ankle in the process of handling the ball. There were four Norwich players in close proximity who were witness to the transgression, and yet only Pukki and Sargent felt the desire to appeal for a penalty; this was more in an insipid manner though, where the referee may actually have thought they were politely enquiring how to go about returning an overdue library book. The decision of the referee was no penalty, with VAR almost instantly agreeing with this.

It became apparent in approximately 60 minutes that the more vociferous and tenacious the manner of appeal is, the more likely the adjudicators will take it seriously and intervene. From a corner kick, we saw a Newcastle header strike the arm (outstretched above his head) of Billy Gilmour, and again the initial official verdict was not to award a penalty. The response from the home team (and in direct comparison to their opponents) was to surround the referee, slapping their hands together like a bob of demented seals, all aggressively demanding a fish. After reviewing the action on the pitch-side monitor, the referee changed his decision – penalty to the ten men.

Widely acknowledged penalty saving expert Tim Krul (who has the honour of being the first substitute goalkeeper in World Cup history to be brought on solely for a penalty shootout – Netherlands v Costa Rica in 2014) got a good hand to Callum Wilson's spot-kick, but the ball went in off the crossbar and Newcastle were in the ascendancy.

Not for the first time this season, it was Pukki to the rescue in the 79th minute with a sumptuous left-footed volley that smashed into the top corner of the net. Pierre Lees-Melou nearly won it for Norwich when he almost capitalised on Schär's error in second-half stoppage time, but the Frenchman was denied by Slovak stopper Martin Dubravka.

The City fans making that long trip home from the 'relegation derby' will have been more than pleased to see their team go four games unbeaten during November but will ultimately feel that 2 points had been dropped in Tyneside.

They were hitting the road again the following Sunday

for yet another inconvenient kick-off time, this time 14:00 at Tottenham's stunning, next-generation stadium on White Hart Lane. To some, the 3-0 defeat was entirely predictable, a wake-up call, a reality check. For example, reporter Michael Bailey being 'brutally honest' on his 'Live Video Verdict' on YouTube, felt that Spurs probably didn't have to get out of second gear to achieve their victory. To others, such as the aforementioned pub landlord who felt a need to knock people's heads off – and let's not forget, a Spurs fan – believed that Norwich could quite easily have got something out of the game and that the score-line was definitely not a true reflection of the 90 minutes that he had seen.

Dean Smith's after-match view concurred with that of the landlord. Speaking to Paddy Davitt of The Pink Un, he thought that his team had created some fine chances, particularly for Pukki, Idah and Sargent and reflected on what could have happened if just one of those had been taken in a timely manner. He went on to say, "Our job, myself and the coaching staff, to make sure these players who have got potential, make sure they start to fulfil it. The likes of Adam, Josh and some of the younger lads we have signed will have to start coming to the party. I have said before we can't be too over-reliant on Teemu. He can score at this level, but we need others to chip in."

City legend Iwan Roberts, also speaking to the Pink Un in 'the big man's weekly column', commented that the three-goal reverse was harsh on his former club and pleaded with the supporters to stick together and 'be supportive'. He, too, referred to the three acceptable chances that had not been taken before, pointedly suggesting that Josh Sargent just didn't look like a natural finisher.

Poor old Josh. Ever since that massive, missed open goal chance against Brighton back in October, he's been in the spotlight for all the wrong reasons. Everyone's aware that he can 'do a job' on the right-hand side of the pitch for Norwich; he's definitely a presence, he's definitely very athletic, he's definitely a very good player outside the constraints of the opponent's penalty area – but he's definitely not doing the business when he can see the whites of the goalkeeper's eyes. It's almost as though one of the opposition, each week, possesses the hidden superpower of Ice Breath, blowing on Sargent as he's in the process of shooting and making him literally freeze in the act. I know, I know.... I've been watching Superman too much.

Iwan (96 goals in 306 Norwich appearances) has perhaps assessed it correctly that Josh is not a 'natural' at finishing. At this relatively early stage of his career, it would be absolutely unfair to compare him with the Welshman who just happens to be the third-highest goalscorer in the club's illustrious history. However, there have been a couple of similar-style chances, such as the ones against Brentford and Newcastle, where he has arrived at the back post, seemingly with the straightforward task of tapping the ball into the net but then inexplicably failing to do so. Is it a general commitment to scoring he lacks, or an in-built determination or just that basic, organic instinct? Whatever the reason, I recall thinking at Brentford that if Iwan had been faced with that particular chance - 2 yards out with the goalie and a defender in close attendance – he would've scored. The whole of Chiswick, Brentford and Kew Bridge, the keeper, the defender, himself and the ball would have ended up in the back of the net. He would have scored.

The fans, Dean Smith, no doubt his teammates (and most obviously Josh himself) are desperate to see him score. I have a vested interest in seeing him get off the mark in the league too – it would hopefully put a stop to the wannabee court jester in front of me in the Main Stand shouting "DON'T GIVE IT TO JIGSAW!" apparently referring to Sargent's penchant for 'falling to pieces in the box'. In a perfect world, that elusive goal would arrive very soon, preferably in the next fixture – Manchester United at Carrow Road.

The Norwich Head Coach had selection issues to contend with leading up to the game, with a mixture of covid-related issues and injuries afflicting his squad. Loanee Brandon Williams was also ineligible to face his parent club. This is not the swaggering, bombastic Manchester United of old though, with the Red Devils class of 2021 currently unable to lay a glove on their biggest rivals and having long since lost their self-styled reputation as the great entertainers. Indeed, in an eye-opening article in the pre-match The Pink Un with opposition fan Gavin Caney, he admitted to United's squad needing a lot of work doing to improve it, with himself and fellow supporters generally having 'given up' on the league already (and remember it's only early December), just hopefully looking forward to the consolation of a good cup run. When asked for his prediction on the game, he thought, 'Norwich are dangerous – they are trying to get a bit of momentum and what will be key to Norwich moving forward is their home form. So this is tough. There won't be a lot in it and it will be edgy, but I fancy United to nick it maybe 1-0'.

Smith had to make five enforced changes to his starting eleven and this was soon to become six as skipper Grant Hanley had to leave the action on 20 minutes with a suspected dislocated shoulder after having being unceremoniously body-slammed to the unforgiving turf by Cristiano Ronaldo. Yet the patched-up Canaries were somehow undaunted by these hindrances in a display full of skill, effort and endeavour, taking the game to their renowned opponents. The returning duo of Giannoulis and Placheta both caught the eye throughout, although arguably the star of the show was Hanley's replacement Jacob Sørensen, the composed and confident Dane belying his total inexperience in the central defensive position.

Unfortunately, the last word had to go to the 36-year-old Ronaldo. The last time he had graced the Carrow Road pitch was way, way back in April 2005, when his team were defeated 2-0. The five-time Ballon d'Or winner is now a very different player from the award-winning version and was feeding off scraps for much of the 90 minutes. However, with the game in its final quarter, he did what he's done very successfully for much of his career; falling down theatrically in the box (this time under a rather innocuous-looking challenge from Max Aarons), arms flailing in the air like he's seriously distressed accompanied by his trademark scream. Compliant referee Darren England pointed to the spot for the softest of penalties which the Portuguese striker duly converted. He sprinted away in celebration (that's Ronaldo, not England) towards the Community Stand corner, wallowing in the adulation of his teammates, seemingly oblivious to the multitude of 'Wanker' and 'V' signs that were coming his way from an unappreciative home faithful. He had 'nicked' the game 1-0, thus proving The Pink Un opposition fan' Gavin Caney, a top tipster in the process.

An irritated Dean Smith stood in the pouring rain, hood most definitely up (resembling a brooding Luke Cage), for his post-match interview. He reflected that his team had gone "toe to toe with another big gun, who wins the game with a dubious penalty", adamant that Ronaldo had made the most of Aaron's challenge. "It's a tough place to come, and Manchester United will be the first to tell you that", he countered, whilst highlighting that visiting keeper David de Gea had been awarded Man of the Match.

He's a strange one that David de Gea, isn't he? There's actually a 12-minute video of him on YouTube titled '*David de Gea's costly errors*' with accompanying commentary such as "David de Gea's made another howler", "David de Gea with a huge error", and "de Gea the fall guy" as he finds different ways and angles to let the ball slip through his hands and through his legs. Sometimes he just doesn't move, rooted to the line like he's momentarily forgotten what he's supposed to be doing, forgotten where he is (a prime example being when Alex Tettey toe-poked one past him at Old Trafford in 2015). He'd certainly had a blinder in his latest game with arms zipping and zapping about all over the place like Spiderman (I know, I know...far too many references to comic book superheroes) with top drawer saves from efforts by Pukki and Kabak.

Despite the disappointment of another defeat, it was again a performance to build on as Smith prepared to welcome his former club Aston Villa to Carrow Road on Tuesday. It would also be the first return to Norfolk for club record sale Emiliano Buendía Stati…

If you happen to be dwelling too negatively on a defeat the day after a game and are in need of a 'pick-me-up', or alternatively need to carry on the celebrations after a stonking win, then there is surely no better place to visit than the Fat Cat & Canary on Thorpe Road as you head eastwards away from the City. This would preferably be accomplished over one of their superb Sunday roasts cooked by the on-site team from Urban Eatery, accompanied by several pints of real ale from the well-stocked bar where there can be up to 5 beers from the Fat Cat brewery plus 7 'guests'.

Originally called the Mustard Pot (named after a Colman's mustard factory steam tug of bygone years), the pub was put up for sale by Adnams brewery in November 2011. After being purchased by Fat Cat supremo Colin Keatley, the pub was ready to be opened under its new guise in May 2012 and has been under the careful management of Christian Hodgkinson ever since.

It must be considered a bit of a coup to have enticed Christian to take on this challenging role at the helm after having filled high-profile positions such as maître d' at Roger Hickman's restaurant (the fine dining establishment on Upper St Giles Street in the City) followed by restaurant manager at the Walpole Arms (now an authentic Spanish tapas eatery set in the heart of the idyllic Norfolk countryside in Itteringham). It is easy to make the assumption that this has worked out well for both parties now as Christian approaches his ten years anniversary as landlord.

It is on Norwich City home match days that the pub is usually at its busiest, attracting a healthy mixture of both Canaries and visitors to this thriving establishment; supporters travelling towards the ground along the busy Yarmouth and Thorpe roads having to pass the 'Canary' as they do. Families are made to feel welcome together with the cask ale and keg enthusiasts seeking out a good pint with the Beer & Burger special offer proving ever popular with many.

Christian can't recollect many tense moments with visiting fans over the last decade, although he wasn't allowed to open, on police instruction, the last time Ipswich came to Carrow Road. They had deemed the immediate area as a place where a flashpoint could certainly occur and even after Christian's objections, they refused to be bowed. It is a decision that he later became thankful for when he was shown video footage of altercations that had consequently taken place!

Until relatively recently, the short 12 minutes walk to the stadium would, for many people, have necessitated passing the intriguingly named drinking establishment The Clarence Harbour - demolished in 2004 to make way for several townhouses to be built. Itself a very popular football supporters venue in its day, the captivating title (according to a 2010 article in the Great Yarmouth Mercury) is a reminder of a once grandiose scheme (named after the Duke of Clarence) nearly two centuries ago to make Norwich an inland port for trade across the North Sea with continental Europe; entry and egress being through

Lowestoft. The Clarence Harbour (the pub, not the port) was constructed in 1837 with the intent of serving those who would build and then subsequently be employed at the new development. Ultimately, the harbour proposal never progressed beyond the drawing board, the emerging railways winning the business with, ironically, Norwich railway station now standing on the originally proposed site. There are still permanent reminders of the innovative plan, however (that would no doubt have transformed mid-nineteenth century Norwich in its own way) with roads still existing in the immediate vicinity titled Clarence, Lower Clarence and Harbour.

Christian is no stranger to this walk to and from the stadium as he is a season ticket holder in the Lower Barclay. There is nothing he likes better than returning to his pub and sampling the cracking atmosphere after the Canaries have won and all his customers are in celebratory mood. However, it was after one such game that there was an incident in the car park that he vividly remembers to this day...a fellow supporter on his way home urgently pulled his car over, seeking vital medical assistance as he was in the throes of a cardiac arrest. CPR was heroically administered by a couple of Fat Cat & Canary regulars for a harrowing 40 minutes before the person was considered to be out of immediate peril. Heart warmingly, he would soon re-visit the pub to offer his gratitude to all involved.

Other than the fine selection of drinks, the splendid Sunday roasts and the nostalgic artefacts portraying Norwich and Norfolk's rich brewing history that are to be enjoyed within the building, it is arguably something on the outer wall that the 'Canary' is currently receiving plenty of publicity for. Back in May 2021, fan group 'Along Come Norwich' commissioned a large mural to be painted on the side of the pub in celebration of the championship-winning feats of the club but in particular those of now ex-Head Coach Daniel Farke. Artist (and fan) Dave Nash, whose working name is Gnasher Murals, took 8 hours to complete the fantastic painting, doing it for free, explaining "it had to be done." It really is an impressive work of art and has created lots of interest, with many supporters having made a special journey to both view it and have photos taken in front of it. Since the German's sacking, there has been concern that it could be covered over as he is no longer in the hot seat – there's no need for them to be worried though, as Christian is determined to keep the painting just as it is as a lasting tribute to Farke's tenure at the club.

So, there I am the day after the Manchester United game in the Fat Cat and Canary. It is, as you would expect, bustling with Sunday afternoon diners and drinkers but probably not as throng as the previous day where not only had the dedicated staff had to deal with match day punters but also employees of Archant Newspapers who were celebrating and promoting the launch of their new The Pink Un app, cutely renaming the pub for 24 hours to the 'Pink Un Free House'. I'm sure all would have had a great time but possibly not as great as mine and the delectable Denise's as we tucked into our succulent roasts.

CHAPTER 9

ASTON VILLA (H)

14TH DECEMBER 2021

I n his pre-match press conference, Dean Smith was adamant that revenge wasn't on his agenda, wanting to steer clear of this specific topic before the fixture against the club that had recently fired him. He was thankful that Norwich City had offered him a chance to get back into football (while confirming that he would always be a Villa fan) and that his sole remit was seeing his new club succeed. He'd been 34 years in football, and only three of those had been with The Villans – he'd actually managed Brentford against them five times and had not been on the losing side once. He knew his old team inside out and was hoping this would work in his favour. He clarified, "I am enjoying life at Norwich, and it just so happens it is Aston Villa on Tuesday. If it was Manchester City or Liverpool, it would be the same. No extra motivation. I can honestly say that. Only the motivation to win the next game."

At the start of the day, the visitors were in 13th place in the table, having lost nine games already, which was just one less than their bottom-of-the-table hosts. However, it soon became obvious that this would be a difficult task for the Canaries when news broke prior to kick-off that nine players were unavailable due to the now customary combination of injuries and covid…

Before the game, it was a pleasure to meet up with my old mate Eoghan in the Lollard's Pit pub, a five-minute walk from Norwich railway station along Riverside Road. It's a rather intriguing name for a hostelry, don't you think? Dig a little deeper though (particularly on the excellent Norfolk Tales, Myths & More website), and it's a title that reveals a grim tale of persecution.

The pub is actually built on the site of an old abandoned pit where chalk workings were primarily dug out to provide foundations for the nearby cathedral, then later utilised as a place where people were burned at the stake for their religious beliefs. The name of the unfortunates was 'Lollard's' (according to the Oxford English Dictionary, the name Lollard is most likely derived from Middle Dutch lollaerd – a mumbler, mutterer – and from the verb lollen – to mutter, mumble). It's possible that it was a derisive expression applied to those without an academic background, educated (if at all) only in English.

Initially, Lollards were followers of a 14th-century English Christian theologian called John Wycliffe, who rose to prominence for translating the bible (usually only available in Latin, the language used by the church and the upper classes) into vernacular English in 1382. He challenged the Catholic Church on numerous points of doctrine and felt that the church had become too institutionalised and corrupt. He wanted to promote a more personal type of Christianity, one that emphasised piety, humility and simplicity. It was a full 40 years after his death that the church declared him a heretic, an event that saw the start of what was concerted persecution of Lollardy over a large area of England. By the mid-15th century, 'lollard' had come to mean a heretic in general.

The greatest concentration of Lollards was to be found in East Anglia, with Norfolk the most influential of hubs due to it being the heartland of the more than restless agricultural peasantry. It was only a matter of time (due to them gaining popular support) before they were subjected to extreme levels of oppression. Firstly in 1410, John Badby (a layman and craftsman) refused to renounce his Lollardy and was burnt, in a barrel, thus becoming the first layman to suffer capital punishment in England for the crime of Heresy.

The Norwich Heresy Trials of 1428-1431 saw 51 men and nine women prosecuted, although not all were condemned to be burnt at Lollard's Pit, with almost half sentenced to public floggings. Persecution of heretics in Norwich then appeared to tail off for a while, only to resurface a century later. As the pit was so conveniently situated just outside the city walls, it was still deemed a suitable place to dispose of those who had been cast out by the church.

The most high profile of these latter burnings was that of Thomas Bilney on 19th August 1531, a Cambridge academic born near Dereham. After primarily having been imprisoned for more than a year in the Tower of London, he was released in 1529 and went back to Cambridge. Here, he was overcome with remorse for his recantations and, after two years, was determined to preach again what he had held to be the truth. As churches were no longer open to him, he mainly preached in fields before finally arriving in Norwich, where Bishop Nix instigated his arrest. After articles were drawn up against him by a large formal assembly, he was tried, degraded from his orders and handed over to the civil authorities to be burned. A parliamentary inquiry then followed, not because they approved of Bilney's doctrine but because it was alleged that his execution had been obtained by the ecclesiastics without the proper authorisation. In 1534 Nix was condemned on this charge resulting in his property being confiscated.

The climax to the burnings at the stake came during the reign of Mary (1553-1558). A commemorative plaque has been placed on the opposite side of the riverbank across the road from the pub, hailing the martyrs who died so horribly in Lollard's Pit all those years ago.

Today, the Lollard's Pit pub is a friendly, cosy, atmospheric freehouse managed by Jonathan' Billy' Barnes. Built somewhere between 1620 and 1670, it was previously called the Kings Arms, then the Bridge House before acquiring its current moniker in 2012. There are usually four reasonably priced real ales on offer from local breweries plus a couple of traditional ciders, with at least one of these from local producer Norfolk Raider. It plays host to many events and gatherings such as ghost hunters, historians, bingo players, pub quiz fanatics and, of course, real ale enthusiasts.

It is in this latter category where Eoghan and I comfortably sit, musing over Norwich's underwhelming season so far while quaffing a couple of pints of Tinsel Toes, the festive offering from Woodforde's Brewery. I used to travel to a lot of the home games with Eoghan's dad Rob (formerly of the Norwich parish but now residing in Chesterfield). I suppose it was a combination of the time of year, the Xmas ale and the fact I was in Eoghan's company that prompted me to think back to a famous carol that his dad had subtly altered the lyrics to in order to pay homage to a certain Norwich player...one that only ended up playing a meagre total of thirteen games in three years at the club, the majority of these being as a late substitute. Yep, he dedicated his carol to the one and only Luciano Becchio, who by his own admission "had a really bad time at the club" after signing from Leeds United in a swap deal, with Steve Morison going in the opposite direction. This didn't perturb Rob though, as Becchio's surname, in his mind, fitted perfectly into the new rhyming couplet...or did it? You see, Rob possesses the broadest Norfolk accent known to man or woman, probably swaying onto the heavy side of the Singing Postman's (ask your grandparents, kids). It went a little something like this:

> *"Oh, the weather outside is frightful*
> *But the fire is so delightful*
> *LEEEEEEEEEDS LET HIM GOOOOOOO ***
> *BECCHIO BECCHIO BECCHIO" ****

* His Norfolk version rhymes with glue.

** Interestingly, he actually rhymed Becchio with snow.

The more Rob had to drink, the more he sang it, and the louder he sang it. In his eyes, he was belting out the Christmas Number One, oblivious to the fact that he started singing it during February after Becchio had signed right at the end of the January 2013 transfer window. Oh, and did I mention that as well as owning the strongest of accents he also happened to be tone-deaf? During one of his virtuoso performances life and soul Paul cast his critical eye over proceedings like an X-Factor judge before proclaiming, "Do you know what Rob, you could sing that song all day long and I guarantee you'd never hit a fucking note." Rob looked Paul in the eye and replied, "I hit all the right notes bor, just not necessarily in the right order."

Eoghan, incidentally, enjoys an even more fabulous accent than his father. Having spent some of his formative years in Ireland, he's acquired the most splendid Irish brogue to add to his natural Norfolk dialect so that he now speaks in a Singing Postman/Shane MacGowan (frontman of The Pogues) intonation. As he's also very expressive and demonstrative with his delivery I thought wouldn't it be wonderful if he could sing 'Fairytale of New York'. "Nooo oi caan' sin", answered Eoghan, disappointingly. Bugger… now that would most definitely be a Christmas Number One!

Before we left for the walk to the stadium, I was made aware of a most fascinating tale linking the pub with one of the victims of those burnings from nearly 500 years ago - Thomas Carmen, who was killed in 1558. Distant relations of his from both the USA and New Zealand had travelled the thousands of miles to visit the Lollard's Pit site and city of their ancestor. Coincidentally, neither the American nor the Antipodean relatives knew of each other's existence until they happened upon the chance meeting in the pub. It most certainly is a small world…

At the final whistle, a dominant Aston Villa had won comfortably. There had been very little to get the Norwich supporters off their seats, with City's overall efforts being sluggish, tired and laboured. It was a totally disheartening display with only an Idah header and a McLean chance worthy of note – the Scot really should have done better when, after anticipating a back pass from Ashley Young, he dinked the ball past the Keeper but with a result similar to that of Sargent's against Brighton. It lacked power and accuracy, enabling a covering defender to easily intercept the ball.

The home crowd went very quiet very quickly, only mutterings and murmurings of discontent to be heard as Tyrone Mings and Buendia patrolled and strutted about the turf like dismissive playground bullies. It was frustrating and horrible to watch in equal measures.

I must admit I'm getting a bee in my bonnet (in truth, there's a swarm of them buzzing about) regarding the whole basic balance of the team. The loanee from Manchester United, Brandon Williams, is obviously a very capable defender (he doesn't half relish a tackle), but he's not at the top of his game when selected at left-back as he's predominantly right-footed. All his good defensive work gets negated as soon as he looks to play the ball down the left flank with his right foot – the ball usually ending up over the touchline for a throw-in to the opponents. I'm not blaming Williams here; he's a young lad very keen to get game time wherever and whenever he can. We are not seeing the best of him though, on his 'wrong side' for many reasons. To exacerbate this issue, tonight we had the chiefly left-footed Przemyslaw Placheta operating down the…yep, you've guessed it, the right-hand side. The result was (the same as with Williams) that on nearly every occasion he got the ball, he cut inside onto his favoured foot with consequently the move coming to a stop. It's similar to listening to a CD that you just know is exasperatingly going to stick after 1 minute 24 seconds of track 5 every…single… time. Aaaaaarrrrggghhhh!!!

There was still hope though, as I was aware that Giannoulis was one of the substitutes. Surely Dean Smith would see sense and bring him on at left-back to improve the balance? I watched him as he warmed up at half-time (with Norwich being a goal behind), away from his fellow subs. He was being instructed to do specific drills by the Fitness Coach while the others walloped balls here, there and everywhere with gay abandon. He didn't look happy though, shaking his head every now and then as though something just wasn't right. Was he injured? Was he unwell? As he never appeared during the second half, I just had to assume that the Head Coach saw a need not to play him.

It was more of the same during the bleak second period as the rain continued to fall. There was always a chance (albeit indeed slim) while the score remained 0-1, but Villa finally put the game to bed with a late second goal by Watkins in the 87th minute. It had been a painful watch.

As I dejectedly trudged out of the stadium into the cold, drizzly night, I began to get my first pangs of concern for our new management team. Were they really up to the job?

Had they just struck lucky in their first few games? There was undoubtedly one factor in their favour; the Aston Villa team that we'd just seen, looking so strong, powerful, positive and athletic, had been pieced together by Smith and Shakespeare. Those particular strengths and impressive traits were seriously needed within the Norwich changing room, and soon. On the flip side, they were now working with a squad of players who they had inherited. Were they capable of positively changing things around, or would it be a challenge akin to shuffling the deckchairs around on the Titanic? Is this why we were seeing square pegs in round holes?

In his post-match press conference, Dean Smith made everyone aware of how difficult the evening had actually been, taking much of the accountability for the seemingly limp effort demonstrated by his team. He explained, "On reflection and in hindsight, I can take responsibility for that because we never really were going at Villa at full tilt, with the players that we would have liked to be going at full tilt. I blame myself really for not pushing to get the game called off because we shouldn't have played."

The Premier League's guidance is that if 13 outfield players and one goalkeeper are available from the players registered in the official 25-man first-team squad, then games will not be postponed.

So, had Norwich been naïve in agreeing to play the game? Information garnered later in the day suggested that this could well have been the case. Firstly we found that an already threadbare squad had been reduced in numbers even further when four players pulled out on the day of the game, plus another three had filled the bench when they were definitely not fit to come on at any time (I assume one of these had to be Giannoulis). Other items worthy of note were:

- Three Academy players (**Jonathan Tomkinson, Tom Dickson-Peters** and **Jon Rowe**) had been named on the bench, with the latter having played a full 90 minutes for the U23s just the previous evening
- **Sam Byram** had made his first senior appearance for the club in 22 months since attaining a hamstring injury in February 2020 against Liverpool. He hadn't been scheduled to make a first-team start until the FA Cup 3rd round match versus Charlton on 9th January
- **Ozan Kabak** should not have been playing (he was substituted for Byram on the stroke of half-time) as he'd recently been suffering from glandular fever and was not up to playing two games in three days
- **Billy Gilmour** had played with a temperature of 38.4 degrees

Norwich City's next fixture at West Ham United's London Stadium was duly postponed due to the obvious lack of numbers. The Villa defeat had felt very damaging though, leaving the team bottom of the pile for Christmas. Only three teams had managed to survive relegation from this position at this time of year since the Premier League began almost thirty years ago.

CHAPTER 10

ARSENAL (H)

26TH DECEMBER 2021

S ituated at the junction of Queens Road and City Road, the Rose Inn has been a favourite pub of Norwich City supporters for many a year. It is also at the back end (or front, depending on your plan of action) of what is an extremely good and substantial pub and food crawl - I know as I do it at least a couple of times a season - that starts with The Champion on Chapelfield Road, followed by The Coachmakers, Trafford Arms, a freshly fried cod from Southwell Fish Bar, Kings Arms, Freemasons, chips (if you're still peckish) from the Golden Fish Bar on Hall Road, before finishing off around the corner at 'the pub on the corner'.

For most fans though, this is their staple pre-match venue of choice, enticed by the five rotating cask ales, several keg beers, plus a well-stocked fridge containing an exceptional selection of canned and bottled products, all of which are from innovative and creative breweries from both this country and overseas. Throw in the fact that the pub supplies a variety of tasty stone-baked pizzas, and it's easy to appreciate and understand the popularity of the place.

First listed as a pub in 1856, the Rose functioned under a succession of brewery ties with the likes of Bullards, Watneys, Courage, and finally Adnams before current owner/operator Dawn Hopkins purchased the premises back in 2003. After briefly closing for a swift cosmetic refurb (mainly consisting of decorating over the garish green & orange colour scheme that Adnams seemed to favour in much of their premises at the time), the doors were back open for customers at the beginning of April, with Dawn keen to provide a community-style pub that offered something different to the norm in this part of Norwich.

She was no stranger to many local connoisseurs of real ale, of course, as she was well known in the City for being landlady of the (now sadly closed, empty and derelict-looking) Ketts Tavern, located at the bottom of Ketts Hill. She had styled this particular establishment on the type of pub that she liked to frequent herself, one that was cosy, comfortable and most importantly, selling real ales. Her early offerings in the 'Ketts' were mainly from the popular local breweries of Woodforde's, Buffy's and Tipple's.

She's also currently no stranger to many Norwich and Norfolk readers of the Eastern Daily Press and Norwich Evening News due to her being Archant's 'go-to' person within the local licensing trade whenever they need a view on such matters, in particular regarding the difficulties that the hospitality trade has recently encountered under restrictions placed on them by the Government during the covid pandemic. Dawn presently holds the prestigious role of Vice Chairman for Campaign for Pubs – a grassroots UK membership organisation that campaigns to support, promote and protect pubs, founded by ex-Liberal Democrat MP Greg Mulholland – and values the opportunity to speak up and air her views via this significant platform.

Arguably, her biggest claim to fame was on the 12th December 2012, when she was selected by CAMRA to address a rally of thousands of people at the London Emmanuel Centre, a short five minute walk from the Houses of Parliament. Calling for MP's to support the pub industry by scrapping the controversial beer tax escalator, she was asked to speak from a publican's point of view, actually sharing the stage with several politicians. It would appear that she enjoyed her 'three minutes of fame' as well. In an article by David Bale printed the following day in the EDP, she said, "It was great to see so many people attend and lobby their MPs on behalf of the pub industry. My three-minute speech also seemed to go down well, and the feedback was really good. I got a good round of applause at the end. It was quite daunting to speak in front of so many people, but they gave us a free pint for Dutch courage just before."

Highly respected and an acknowledged ambassador for the pub trade in Norwich, Dawn was now familiar with meeting politicians as a few months prior to the rally in London, she had also visited the capital for an annual Labour party business reception in the company of Ed Milliband and future Norwich City FC chairman Ed Balls. Invited due to her heavy involvement in the successful Norwich City of Ale event, she hoped her links with the latter would keep the plight of struggling publicans foremost in their minds. Intriguingly (bearing in mind this event was nearly ten years ago), she wanted to discuss issues surrounding business rates, the beer duty escalator, supermarkets selling cheap booze and the problems she and other publicans faced with the increased costs of employing staff – all problems that are still currently applicable, no doubt.

Today, an hour or so before kick-off against Arsenal, the Rose is still quite throng but not so packed as is my usual experience on a match day. It is Boxing Day though, there is no public transport, and maybe people have decided to stay at home with their families; then again, they may have spent up over the Xmas period, or they may have prematurely given up on the Canaries. Who knows? Outside, it's also generally on the quieter side as I make my way to the stadium; there's a lot fewer cars and people milling about this busy road than normal.

There are two main, popular routes from this part of the City to Carrow Road. The first is the Southgate Lane knee cracker that I mentioned in the Southampton (H) chapter, while the second is down the more joint-friendly, less stressful Carrow Hill. In the middle of these favoured paths, there happens to be a third, rarely ever used course that I treat myself to every so often. Just on Carrow Hill, to the left after leaving Queens Road, is what looks like a private driveway to a rather large house – it's not though; it actually leads to a public pathway that transports you into an enchanted, long forgotten, lost kingdom. It's also where you'll find the finest, most intact section of the City's medieval fortifications. I've yet to meet anyone along here, and yet it's a treasure trove of spectacular architecturally complex, walled defences made up of knapped and squared flint, awash with diverse shapes and structures. There's a cacophony of towers (including the fantabulous Black Tower), fascinating and alluring doorways, parapets, chambers, turrets, stairways, fireplaces, formidable and imposing archways, plus more putlogs than you can shake your bow and arrow at.

It's not hard to imagine that in other parts of the world, there would now be a theme park here, an information building advertising 'Book here for the City Walls experience', an ice-cream parlour, a selection of coffee shops, a souvenir shop selling over-priced tea-towels, pencils, badges and photocopied fact-finding sheets for £1. There would undoubtedly be a fast food outlet selling their 'Mega Tower Burger'.

At the moment, as usual, there is not a soul to be seen. Yes, it's raining, it's muddy in parts along the deep, steep steps, but I don't care – it's magical. I walk around the bend of the last tower near to where two paths converge to be greeted by the sheepish grin of an Arsenal fan who's decided he's found an opportune time and place to have a piss. "Sorry, mate" he says as I harrumph my way past him, ensuring I avoid the backsplash off those special walls built to protect the City of Norwich 700 years ago.

As the Omicron variant of covid continues to wreak havoc on society (today alone, there's a reported 103,558 new cases), there are plenty of empty yellow seats to be seen in the stadium with infected people having to isolate or alternatively steering well clear in a justified attempt to remain safe. It turns out to be a good game to miss as just after five minutes I hear myself involuntary groan (confirmation that this season is gradually turning me into a

City Stand Victor Meldrew – I genuinely don't want to be that person) as Norwich City left-back, Brandon Williams needlessly bends the ball out of play, with his right foot, for a throw in to the visitors. He wasn't under any undue pressure, just a routine attempted pass to a colleague down the left flank, gifting possession away. Arsenal swiftly and skilfully work the ball over to the opposite side of the pitch before briefly losing the ball themselves, only to immediately regain it as Ozan Kabak fails to find Max Aarons. There are then a further 11 (yes, ELEVEN) opposition touches before Angus Gunn is picking the ball out of the back of his net. He too, will think he could've, should've done better. It's only 6 minutes into the 90, and it's Norwich 0 Arsenal 1, the rot's already set in, the confidence of players and fans shot, the game is over.

To make matters worse, we are then subjected to the bizarre and disheartening sight of midfielder Kenny McLean issuing the most public of bollockings to centre-half Kabak for having given the ball away. He's aggressively in his face; he's apparently telling him he should have just launched the ball down the other end of the pitch, out of the ground, anywhere. He's seemingly telling him (while also letting 25,000-plus supporters know in this unedifying process) that it's his fault alone that Norwich are one goal down. At the Watford game back in September, we'd seen the team 'conducting a very public inquest, pointing 'the finger of blame' at colleagues followed by a slumping of the shoulders and a bowing of the heads' but nothing like this in an act more in keeping with a local Sunday league pub game where everyone's still beered up from the night before.

I fleetingly amuse myself by imagining Kabak picking McLean up by the ears at arm's length, with the much smaller overly-angry Scot exasperatingly lashing out with arms and legs - in a flurry of fake puffs of cloud - unable to hit his intended target like he's a character in a Warner Bros Looney Tunes cartoon. The Turkish international then launches Kenny over the touchline where, on impact with the turf, he stares into the camera; his big wide eyes slowly start to crack into fragments, then fall to the ground in a heap of pebbles. Kabak the Victor stands to one side, a triumphant grin on his face.

Back in the real world, and Kenny's still at it. Players and fans from both teams are now staring on in bemusement as Norwich wait to kick off after the goal. Kabak stands there crestfallen. Mercifully, after what seems like an eternity, skipper Gibson intervenes and eventually manages to usher the aggressor away. This is Kenny McLean, let's remind ourselves, with a 2021/2022 Premier League record so far of zero goals and zero assists – he does occasionally head a dangerous corner away though, I suppose.

In truth, it's a doddle for the north Londoners as they pick their opponents off with ease, striking out comfortably with their weakening jabs. In attempted retaliation, Norwich are unable to lay a glove on them. Just before half-time, there's surprisingly a bit of argy-bargy in front of the dugouts, raising us home supporters out of our stupor, like the drunken Uncle the previous day who's been woken up after his Xmas dinner to watch his favourite James Bond film. We're soon slinking back into our seats as Tierney cuts in from the left to fire in via the far post to give his side a 2-0 half-time lead. He could not have expected any more room if he had stood on a deserted West Runton beach.

The pedigree Gunners manage to score three more in the second stanza as the bedraggled Canaries look sorry for themselves in what is a hapless performance. It's staggering to reflect that in the corresponding fixture at the Emirates Stadium, Arsenal were actually propping up the table. They're totally ruthless as well. There's a term in football called 'Shit-housery' (e.g. think Newcastle players surrounding the referee in order to gain a penalty a few weeks ago), and I appreciate it is nothing new. It is fair to say Arsenal are shit-hot at 'Shit-housery', with Bukayo Saka, a master of the art at the tender age of 20. His trademark act is, when successfully tackled, he falls to the floor clutching his ankle with one hand, the other arm waving in distress (think Ronaldo). He wants a free kick, but the referee has not adjudicated the tackle as a foul. There's a bit of a distraught roll around (he's seriously hurt here, don't forget) as, by now, his team have easily regained possession. Everyone's looking over at him; is he ok or not? The games in limbo as Arsenal finally boot the ball into touch so their colleague can urgently receive medical attention – there's no need though, as he makes a miraculous recovery, jumping to his feet in a sprightly manner before limping away for the next five yards – it's classic, high-level 'Shit-housery'. Norwich are not even entry-level standard as they continue to submissively throw the ball back to their opponents. I can understand this on the first occasion; I'm having serious doubts the second time, but on the third? Come on City, keep the ball!

I've got a mate called Billy who's an honest chap. He

likes a drink does Billy, and on a recent visit to his local surgery for his annual health check was asked by his GP how much alcohol he usually drank each week. "As much as I fucking can", answered my friend. No trying to pull the wool over anyone's eyes here. "I appreciate your honesty," said the startled Doc. I've got Dean Smith down as being the honest type as well. Speaking after the game on his club's official YouTube channel, he admits to being bitterly disappointed with the performance but that his overriding emotion is one of anger (I can see he's clearly agitated as he keeps alternating his standing position from one foot to the other – he can't stand still). He hadn't seen that performance coming; training had been OK but there had been too many unforced errors. He wanted to see more drive and admitted that standards had dropped since his first few games. Regarding the forthcoming game at Crystal Palace, he thought it was ridiculous that another fixture had been scheduled in just 48 hours time. Although he understood the Xmas traditions, he emphasised that these were unique circumstances at the moment, with covid pushing players to the limit. He then confirmed that not one player who had missed the Arsenal match through the virus or injury would come into contention for the trip to Palace's none-too-palatial Selhurst Park home...

Angus Gunn was again picking the ball out of the onion bag within the first 10 minutes after a needless challenge, by that man Kenny McLean, had gifted Palace a penalty. The mischievous side of me willed Ozan Kabak (today, he's a substitute) to come onto the field and admonish the fiery Scot in a warranted act of retribution, but it wasn't to be. The Eagles put the game to bed with two further goals before the interval, with the visitors leaving the field for their half-time cuppa with cries of "You're not fit to wear the shirt" ringing in their ears. The fans had started to turn.

There was a brief moment of light relief as gallows humour made an appearance after the break as the travelling supporters entertained themselves by singing "Let's pretend we've scored a goal" – it was now well over seven very long hours since Teemu Pukki had scored that late leveller at Newcastle.

Later on, as the game meandered towards the final whistle, events, unfortunately, started to take a huge turn for the worse as a pocket of supporters vented their dissatisfaction with the Canaries' recent performances by advising young loanee Billy Gilmour to return to his parent club, Chelsea (but not exactly in those words if you get my drift). Throw in the fact that rookie striker Adam Idah announced that he'd been racially abused on his Instagram account (plus there were reports that a couple of Crystal Palace players had also been subjected to the same type of sinister abuse), and it had been the most desperate of days in the club's long and memorable history.

Regarding the racism, The Canaries Trust was pleasingly quick to issue the following early evening statement: "The Trust utterly condemns the appalling racist and personal abuse suffered by some of our players on social media this evening. Regardless of performances on the pitch, this is completely unacceptable. We urge the club and police to take appropriate action."

Meanwhile, former Glasgow Rangers and Scotland star Barry Ferguson, was one of a host of people to come out in support of Gilmour. Speaking to the Daily Record, he urged the 20-year-old to respond in the right way by doing his talking on the pitch, before adding, "It just sickened me when I saw it. It's baffling. Some people just don't appreciate good footballers. I've said it numerous times; he's just a wonderful player. The response from the Norwich crowd annoyed and frustrated me; it made me angry. I am convinced Gilmour will go on to become one of the best midfielders in Britain. It's not a pleasant thing to go through. I've been there myself, and no one likes criticism. But you can use it as a positive and throw it back in their faces."

As the current month and year approached their final days, stats guru website 'Opta Joe' informed us 'Norwich in December 2021 are the first-ever Premier League side to lose at least five games and fail to score a goal within any month in any year in the competition's history'. Crikey, I wonder how 'stats don't lie' Benjamin is feeling about that sorry state of affairs.

Another stat I am informed of is that Dean Smith has never been relegated while he has been a Head Coach. His current team now require snookers, 37 off the last over, a hole-in-one at the 18th if he is to keep that envious record intact.

CHAPTER 11

EVERTON (H)

15TH JANUARY 2022

Happy New Year! A time to switch off, reboot, then press that metaphorical personal reset button. We've come across hard (footballing) times these last five months or so, but things can only get better, can't they? Nothing actually forces us into a more positive frame of mind as a turbulent end of one year stumbles over the step into a new one. In its own unique way, it's ambiguous; just the turning over of a page on the calendar or the single tick or tock of a clock, but time is indeed passing as always.

Some people have a weird, long-held tradition that they have to illogically adhere to in order to hopefully induce better luck from the gods during the forthcoming twelve months. For example, while I was still a teenager and living with my ordinarily rational parents, they insisted that their black cat had to be the last living creature out of the back door before the clock struck 12. It was also a bizarre necessity that it also had to be the first living creature back through said door afterwards. Now, this wasn't as easy a task as you may imagine, as the cat did not always want to play ball. Just imagine, it's contentedly sprawled out in front of the fire, on its favourite antimacassar, and my Dad's trying to lever him off it at five minutes to midnight and out into the frosty night - the feline's not having it. After a brief struggle though, it's the first part of the mission accomplished as the cat grumpily and somewhat tentatively stretches out into the dark, icy air. Successfully getting it quickly back in just a few minutes later was nigh on an impossibility. Clearly narked, it had gone off in search of a better offer leaving my freezing parents standing out in the back yard shouting "Roger, Roger" – I'd named him after 70's City striker Roger Gibbins – "Come on, we've got some of your favourite chicken." After a while, I'd arrive on the scene, bladdered and no help whatsoever after taking part in a mass, alcohol-fuelled fancy dress party in my local village. All I wanted to do was to go to bed (no doubt after consuming the entire contents of the fridge), but no, I wasn't allowed through the door until good luck charm Roger had decided to grace our presence once more. I could imagine him sitting behind a bush, moodily observing us gradually turn a deeper shade of blue, thinking, "You lot can fuck right off. You can wait a bit. Plus, while I'm at it, what's that gormless tool doing dressed as a pirate."

I do not know if Dean Smith has any New Year rituals that he performs, but he would undoubtedly be hoping for a better run of luck as 2022 commenced, particularly with illnesses and injuries within his squad. The first scheduled fixture of the year against Leicester City had already been postponed with the Premier League issuing a rather formal statement: 'Following a request from Norwich City, the Premier board met today and regrettably agreed to postpone the club's fixture at Leicester City's King Power Stadium, due to be played at 1500GMT on Saturday 1 January. The board accepted Norwich's application as the club does not have the required number of players available for the match (13 outfield players and one goalkeeper) due to Covid-19 cases and injuries. The decision by the board was able to be made in advance of the fixture to give clarity to the affected clubs and their fans. We apologise for the inconvenience and disruption caused to supporters' festive plans'. Don't you worry about that, my old sausages. We'd rather have the 'inconvenience and disruption' rather than another unnecessary dry humping. This was Norwich City's personal switch-off and reboot moment; a chance for players, staff and fans to recover, a collective opportunity to lick the wounds.

The first competitive match of the year, therefore, was an FA Cup third-round tie at The Valley, home of Division 1 Charlton Athletic FC. A few familiar faces did indeed return to the starting line-up (Krul and Hanley), while a couple of other returnees (Pukki and Rashica) had to settle for a place on the bench. It's fair to say it was a rather strange afternoon. Norwich couldn't get going during the first 45 minutes, enduring a difficult first half with the home team having much the better of proceedings. Pukki and Rashica entered the fray at the break, combining in the 79th minute for the latter to score the winner (his first goal for the club). I say 'a rather strange afternoon' because there was a healthy, very noisy travelling contingent of away fans in attendance, but many of the chants had a sardonic, ironic or (potentially) toxic edge to them. Also, a couple of banners were on display, one of which was an instruction for a co-owner 'DELIA, SELL THE CLUB' while the other stated 'NO AMBITION NO FIGHT DELIA OUT'. During the 90 minutes, does this help? Will the team play any better hearing the negative chants and observing the banners? We already know from Southampton's James Ward-Prowse that he truly believed that supporters had made a positive difference during the Canaries' home win in November when he admitted 'the fans definitely played a big part in spurring their team on'.

On the other hand, a relatively new chant, dedicated to scorer Milot Rashica, had caught the imagination of fans. A jazzy, enormously upbeat version of the tune 'Tequila' reached an almighty crescendo after the goal. The Kosovan international said afterwards, "I haven't heard it for four or five weeks, but it's nice to hear it back. I hope we will hear it more in the future." See, they do listen; they do hear what the supporters have to say.

Dean Smith had definitely heard the adverse chanting and was none too pleased. When asked for his views on them, prior to the upcoming re-scheduled fixture at West Ham United, he said, "I'll be honest, I don't like the sarcasm from the fans. We need to be together. There are reasons for our performances in the last three matches. I would urge them to get behind us. I'd rather fans show their frustration after the game rather than during, especially given some players are suffering from a lack of confidence." It was clear that the fans' celebrations of imaginary goals and triumphant chants of 'We've had a shot' had gone down like a lead balloon with the management. Smith continued, "I know at times it is only a minority, but I would ask them to refrain from that and get behind us, and hopefully, we can give them something to shout about. It was only a few games ago that I was being told by Norwich fans that our performance against Manchester United was up there with top performances. So hopefully, we can get back there, and with the supporters, we can all be pulling in the same direction." He acknowledged it had not been an easy time to stay positive, reiterating, "I totally understand frustrations. Because we're in a battle at the moment, I'd like their frustrations to be vented at the end rather than during the game."

Talksport then entered the scene (of course they did, always happy to stick the boot in), this time via Simon Jordan, a businessman who made his fortune in the mobile phone industry (in 2000, he'd purchased Crystal Palace FC and remained chairman of the club until they entered administration in early 2010). Commenting on Dean Smith's response to the antagonistic chanting, in a scathing attack, he said, "They've been awful. They have been a disgrace. They are so poor. I like Norwich and I like Dean Smith, but you're defending the indefensible by saying that the supporters don't have a right to be vitriolic. They are scandalously bad. Make a performance that makes them (City fans) stop doing it because they are rubbish. I don't think it's ideal, but you reap what you sow. They are embarrassed by it. I've got no dog in the fight. I like Norwich, I'm a big fan of Delia's and I like the ownership of the club. I like the club full stop, but you've got to call things for what they are – they are absolutely crap." Thanks for that insight, Simon. I think we can quite comprehensively say that usurps anything that Messrs O'Hara, Crook and Ashton have collectively commented this season.

Alternatively, West Ham fans were cock-a-hoop with their teams' current performances and league position so far and were feeling rather optimistic. A quick scan before the game through the fan's message-board 'Knees Up Mother Brown' featured several excessively positive score predictions, such as from SullySpecial with '8-0 to West Ham' while Georgee Paris went three better with 'We will win 11-0'. Arguably, the most surprising comment was reserved for 'hammers92', who stated, 'I'm rather happy to lose this one 5-0 if it means we beat Spurs midweek to be honest'. In fairness, these were all posted before the original postponed fixture, but there was no reason to suggest the views had changed with West Ham still on a decent run of form and also through to the next round of the FA Cup after dispatching those pesky Peacocks from Leeds.

The Hammers ultimately and predictably beat The Canaries 2-0. The 90 minutes were similar to the Everton (a) fixture back in September where City had been competitive, the defensive performance had been more solid, but this had possibly had an impact on creative output as there was little threat up front. Gary Gowers from the 'MyFootballWriter' website summed it up with the following key points and observations:

Bog standard #ncfc Premier League defeat
Powderpuff going forward
Fragile at the back

Lots of nothingness in middle third
Can we declare? What a miserable season

Do you know what though? Believe it or not, there was actually another team in the Premier League who had hit the skids recently; and they just happened to be Norwich's next opponents at Carrow Road – the underperforming Toffees of Everton FC.

A pre-match article appeared in The Guardian the day before the fixture. Titled 'A bad week to get worse for Everton' and, penned by Barry Glendenning, it explained, "After seeing their team win just one game and draw three from their past 12 Premier League outings, Everton supporters are mutinous. This week's sale of their talented French left-back Lucas Digne to Aston Villa, in the wake of his reported falling-out with Rafa Benitez, is likely to have further enraged a fanbase whose patience with their manager was already wearing cigarette paper-thin. 'Sometimes it only takes one person from outside to destroy a beautiful love affair' wrote Digne in what has widely been perceived as a dig at his former manager. With Benitez's side heading to Carrow Road to face an abominably bad Norwich City side on Saturday, anything less than emphatic victory would further damage the already fractious relationship between Everton fans and their manager."

So, could we (ahem) lick the Toffees and give Everton a dose of the January blues? I was certainly feeling bright and enthusiastic as I boarded the 06:19 Northern Trains service from Chesterfield to Nottingham on the first section of my journey to the Fine City. I'd successfully navigated my way around the last of the severely under-the-influence early morning revellers ("let's fucking get a fucking taxi") falling out of the extremely late bars on my approach to the station, mesmerised as usual by the thought that I was just beginning my day stone-cold sober as others were completing theirs after a night of excess.

I was joined on the train once again by the Nottingham Forest fans I'd seen prior to our game against Southampton, who today were on their way to Millwall. I'm pleased to report there were no first-hand accounts of OCD related locked-door checking this time. The issue on this occasion was a couple of them were not happy with the direction they were sitting; they wanted to sit with their backs to the driver, definitely not wanting to face the front. As the re-arrangement amongst friends gathered pace in order to accommodate their request to move, they were asked was this because they suffered from travel sickness? "No, it's just better karma sat this way and gives Forest a better chance of winning."

"What a load of old baloney that is," I thought, before casually altering my own seat position, hoping to give my team a hand later that afternoon, doing my bit for the cause and all that.

Later that morning, as the train trundled through the outer edges of the Norwich suburbs, my phone rang. "Kid, I woke up this morning and decided I want to go to the game." It was only life and soul Paul, 'back in the room' for the first time in two months!

We eagerly made our way to one of our favourite hostelries - the Louis Marchesi - which stands prominently and proudly on the Tombland/Wensum Street corner, directly opposite the Maids Head Hotel. But who is this chap that the pub is named after, I hear you ask? Well, thanks for inquiring. Erminio William Louis Marchesi (to give him his full moniker) was the person who founded the Round Table movement in Norwich in 1927, an international fellowship and community charitable organisation for young men (motto 'Adopt, Adapt, Improve). Interestingly, this was the building chosen for many group meetings after formation.

Dating from 1771, the pub was built on the site of an earlier 14th-century construction (of which the crypt still survives). Predominantly a rather bland-looking structure, it was originally called the Waggon & Horses (the lane next to the pub still carries this name), and it was not until 1902 that owners and local brewers Steward and Patteson followed the Edwardian trend of creating the Tudor-style, exposed timber frontage of the 'Louis' that we are so familiar with today. In 1976, the name 'Louis Marchesi' was adopted for the first time in the man's honour, then altered again in 2004 to 'Take 5' – I suspect that this title was due to the (then) owners being ardent followers of the American jazz pianist Dave Brubeck, and not that they were overly partial to taking short naps during the afternoon.

By 2017 the 'Take 5' had begun to lose its way a little and required some much-needed impetus and TLC - enter local entrepreneur Lisa Atkins, who took on the ownership and immediately changed the name of the grade II listed premises back to 'Louis Marchesi', not only bringing back to life a previous name but also the fortunes of this much-loved venue.

It was a key component of many a City night out 'back in the day' of course, due to its adjacent proximity to the

Sansom & Hercules/Ritzy's nightspot, and even though the doors have long since been closed next door, it still retains its popularity, especially on football match days. Today's game is no different as Paul and I enter a packed interior, and it's easy to see what punters are lured by due to Lisa having expertly utilised the whole of the premises:

- The main bar area is in the style of an old-fashioned pub that contains a few modern twists. It's convivial, sociable, welcoming and features comfy sofas and a lovely open fire. Ales, ciders and gins from local producers are available amongst a very good overall selection of drinks.
- The Undercroft (in the 14th-century crypt) hosts parties, wine, rum and gin tastings, acoustic nights, business meetings, choirs, actors and poetry meetings. It's also a games room, so if you don't fancy any of the above, you could always lose your marbles by playing Connect 4 or Jenga – other frustrating games are available.
- First Floor, which opens out onto a terrace, is also available for private functions.

It's Paul's round, and he orders a pint of lager for him and a pint of Tobi's Tipple (a soft and fruity real ale from Moongazer-Norfolk Brewhouse) for me. We have an immediate issue as he's insisting on a branded glass for his drink to be served in, but the somewhat flustered bar staff have run out of them already. They only have the standard pint pots available. Lisa arrives on the scene and politely and cheerily enquires as to what the problem is: "I want my lager in a branded glass, and you've not got any. If you yourself ordered a red wine, you wouldn't want it served in any old pint pot would you?" queries a clearly disgruntled Paul. Lisa's suitably streetwise though, and has developed the necessary customer service skills to deal with such occurrences. With a sparkle in her eye and a smile on her lips, she considers the question for a moment before thoughtfully replying, "Oh, I don't know...sounds like rather a good idea to me!" A masterclass in diffusing what could have been an awkward situation.

A while later, I entered the stadium, where I was met by two sets of supporters who were possibly expecting the worse over the course of the next one hour and thirty minutes. It certainly felt on the quieter side; both Norwich and Everton fans were making an effort but not creating the amount of noise that had been generated by the hordes much earlier in the season. This was all to gloriously change (for those of a yellow & green persuasion) in the 16th minute as Blues defender Michael Keane, conscious of Adam Idah lurking over his shoulder, stretched to cut out Josh Sargent's low cross and instead diverted it past a helpless Jordan Pickford to give City the lead. Within 94 seconds, with the Barclay End joyfully and/or sardonically singing 'We've scored a goal', Idah made it two with his first Premier League goal, poking home following a pinpoint pass from Brandon Williams at the end of a barnstorming run.

Everton fans were distraught. They too had banners of protest demanding 'BENITEZ GET OUT OF OUR CLUB' and 'SACK THE BOARD'. Norwich fans were delirious, mocking the Toffees manager by singing "You're getting sacked in the morning", with his own clubs' fans zealously joining in. Then we had an angry pitch invader from the visitor's section of the ground. He looked like he was attempting to make his way over to remonstrate with Benitez on the opposite side of the pitch, but a combination of unsuitable leisure-wear trainers and maybe an inappropriate pre-match diet effectively contributed to him being apprehended by a fleet-footed steward way before he'd even reached the sunlit lands of the centre circle.

Substitute Richarlison pulled a goal back for his team, but Norwich somehow found the strength of character and the quality of play to put an end to the run of six consecutive league defeats. Everton had the better of the second half but not to the extent to which City had dominated the first and, odd as it was for us fans to see, managed the game out well to claim a much-prized victory.

Pleasingly, there were also a couple of delicious 'Shit-housery' moments towards the end of the game. First of all, we witnessed Williams (who'd had a storming game) ambling his way off the field, with a bit of a pantomime limp to boot, it must be said, to be substituted with Sam Byram. Everton's towering Columbian centre half Yerry Mina (a reported 6ft 4in to Williams's 5ft 6in) clearly took umbrage to this, rushing over to the City defender to hasten his departure. Judging by his actions, I'm pretty sure Mina's exact words weren't, "Come on, Brandon, old chap, could you possibly hurry off the field as quickly as you can please, as my team are desperately trying to secure an equaliser" but I guess we'll never know. The spirited Williams was not having any of it anyway, belligerently brushing his aggressor off, before making his way to the touchline in his own time.

The most spontaneous act of 'Shit-housery' came from a fellow fan in the Main Stand. After catching a stray clearance, instead of throwing the match ball back down for the throw-in to be taken as is the norm, he walked down the stairway step by glorious step in an attempt to wind down the clock before personally handing the ball back. It was almost as if he should claim an assist for contributing to his team getting the three points, and as Dean Smith had earlier pleaded, 'we need to be together'.

The following day Rafa Benitez was indeed sacked. The Liverpool Echo reporter, Chris Beesley, fascinatingly pointed out that there had been a similar scenario in November 2019 when Norwich's fans had sang the same 'Getting sacked in the morning' ditty to then Everton boss Marco Silva - who was himself fired shortly afterwards – during City's 2-0 victory. However, later in the day, we were informed on Twitter (by *UpperGwladysBlue*) that the Canaries actually had a greater stranglehold on bosses of the Goodison Park club than first imagined. The tweet highlighted:

- *'The curious trend of Norwich ending EFC managerial reigns*
- *Kendall 1 – last away game at Norwich*
- *Walker – last game Norwich away*
- *Royle/Unsy caretakers in May 2016 – last game Norwich at home*
- *Silva – last home game Norwich*
- *Benitez – last game Norwich away*
- *Spooky!'*

The next Everton FC manager, whoever it may be, would surely be heartened to know that as his new team had already played the Canaries twice this season, his tenure would be safe for at least the next seven months.

CHAPTER 12
CRYSTAL PALACE (H)
9TH FEBRUARY 2022

Norwich fans were delirious as their team went two goals up, mocking the opposition's manager by singing "You're getting sacked in the morning", with his own clubs' fans accommodatingly joining in. However, just wait a minute – this wasn't Everton's Rafa Benitez's managerial status we're still speculating on. It's actually Claudio Ranieri of Watford's unfortunate turn under the brightest of Friday night spotlights, and it's becoming more than apparent that if you're a boss whose team loses to Norwich, you strongly face the possibility of getting fired.

Watford FC (not satisfied with one nickname, they've got five – The Hornets, The Golden Boys, Yellow Army, The 'Orns and, last but not least, The Prolific Manager-Sackers) have been owned by the Pozzo family since 2012. They certainly don't hang around when it comes to pulling the plug on managerial regimes. With a 'get results, or you're gone' ethos, if we include Javier Gracia, whose first day in the very-hot seat was on the 21st of January 2018, they have had eight managers in a four-year period. I'm no mathematician, but even I can calculate that means, on average, you'll get the best part of six months in the job before collecting your P45. At this swift rate of knots, there's undoubtedly a very good chance that, come the end of the season, both the manager who replaces Ranieri AND the one who replaces his replacement a few months later could also be gone. A sack first/think later culture if ever there was one (and Ranieri was duly relieved of his duties on the Monday following the game, to be replaced by Roy Hodgson, whose appointment Watford were 'delighted' to announce).

Anyway, let's get back to the match, the 100th league game between these two teams. It was a night when (ahem) Sargent finally earnt his stripes as (ahem) the lights went out for Watford in more ways than one as the Canaries (ahem) took the sting out of the Hornets with a 3-0 victory. Phew, and that's it for the puns…honest.

For City's opening goal, there was much to admire and applause has to be given to the imperious referee, Mike Dean. Firstly, he didn't fall for the spectacular tumble by home defender Samir who was being tracked by a determined and ever-willing Pukki. The Finn retrieved the ball just before it went over the goal line, looked up and saw the onrushing Sargent who, with the ball arrowed slightly behind him, produced an exquisite, improvised scorpion-like kick that sent the ball towards the underside of the crossbar and over the line for his first-ever Premier League strike, thus sparking wild celebrations in the visiting fans enclosure. A few things for VAR to check there then, but when the decision eventually arrived to confirm the goal, it was a joy to witness a vindicated Dean point to the centre spot with a superb, amateur-dramatic flourish, delighted that his decision-making had been proved to be correct.

A temporary power cut then called a halt to proceedings as approximately 50 per cent of the floodlights tripped, leaving the ground in partial darkness. The two teams had already devised a subtle, cunning plan to cover for such eventualities, however, as they both were wearing shirts that can only be described as atomic-luminous, a serious threat to the retinas but near perfect for dimmed illumination. Watford favoured a garish, stark yellow while Norwich sported their change kit that is officially described as 'fluorescent coral'. These are so bright that not only could they easily be seen from the Vicarage Road terraces, but there were also unconfirmed reports that there had been sightings from the moon. Both sets of supporters also lent a hand as City fans, scenting a rare away triumph, flashed their mobile telephone lights while the home team's followers, of which Sir Elton John is one, were reduced to waving (ahem) candles in the wind (OK....I know, I know).

When play resumed, Sargent notched his second with a thumping far post header from Rashica's left-wing cross. The game was finally put to bed when Watford's substitute Juraj Kucka decided it was an ideal time to impersonate Everton's Michael Keane (from the previous weekend) by stretching to cut out Adam Idah's low cross and instead diverting it past a forlorn Daniel Bachmann. City had consequently doubled their away goals tally for the season within the course of one evening.

The result moved the Canaries out of the bottom three

for the first time this campaign, and as the latest enforced break came into view, the fans of *The Hornets, Golden Boys, Yellow Army,'Orns and Prolific Manager-Sackers* congratulated their visitors by singing "You're going down with the Watford", thus proving that Norwich City do not have the monopoly on fans taking the mickey out of their own team.

Another scheduled 'break' was then factored into Premier League proceedings following a somewhat packed and yet heavily disrupted schedule. This time it was officially classed as the winter variant, although there were international matches taking place (such as in the African Cup of Nations and World Cup Qualifiers in South America and Asia), just not ones involving UEFA-affiliated countries. I must admit to this one catching me on the hop – I had just assumed my personal football season was once again being disrupted for yet another unnecessary, inconsequential, lop-sided England fixture against Nicaragu-akhstan-arino, or whoever it is that they usually play in these types of games.

You'd imagine that a scheduled break would be welcomed by the Archant people dedicated to penning articles (seemingly 24/7) on Norwich City FC for the Eastern Daily Press and Norwich Evening News; an ideal time for downing laptops for a few days and recharging the mental, physical and mechanical batteries maybe. Speaking to the genial Paddy Davitt (Football Editor), this is far from the case due to City fans having an insatiable thirst for news on their beloved club – such as me, I suppose, when I have the unfathomable urge for wanting to read his match report (for a game I've just personally witnessed) immediately after the referee's blown the final whistle.

The Canaries, being the only club in the county of

Norfolk in the top four divisions, pride themselves on pro-actively trying to provide information for the fan base, particularly regarding their cultural philosophy, whereas other clubs are definitely seen as being more guarded. However, there has still got to be slow news days whatever the time of year, and I've spotted a couple of EDP headlines (that are not attributed to Paddy) in the recent past where this could possibly be the case. For example, on the 10th of April 2021, there was this:

'Peter Crouch drove to Yarmouth while on Norwich loan – and wasn't impressed'

Now I'm pretty sure Crouchy's not the only person to have visited the east coast resort town over the years and not been totally enthralled by the place, so this is not that much of an earth-shattering revelation. Plus, take a note of the date of the article; this was over 17 years since his loan spell had concluded at Carrow Road in December 2003.

Here's another from the 23rd of April 2021:

'Mystery of the missing Daniel Farke portrait is solved!'

Local artist John Etheridge had finally received confirmation that his painting had been received by the then Norwich boss. Here's the thing - he'd posted it on the 17th of August 2020. Why had it taken eight months for him to find out?

This is definitely my gold medal winner though, from the 5th of June 2021:

'Bus services delayed following reports of yacht in tree'

This followed a tweet from local company Konectbus apologising to local service users that 'Route 6, 13:42 Wymondham to Watton is currently running 30 mins late due to being stuck behind a Yacht in a tree!! apologises (sic)'. Well, I guess it beats 'leaves on the line' in a game of public transport Top Trumps…

There was, of course, a break of the unscheduled type at the commencement of the covid pandemic after the game at Sheffield United played on the 7th of March 2020. The next game did not take place until over three months later when Southampton visited Carrow Road on the 19th of June. This was not as big an issue for Paddy and his associates as you would imagine as they implemented processes and techniques that they were familiar with during a routine pre-season, such as the sure-fire winner of interviewing ex-players with interesting stories to tell. They also became more creative, such as adapting to watching iconic City games from history with colleagues in an entertaining and engaging 'Gogglebox' format.

Paddy is the first to acknowledge that he benefits from enjoying a healthy relationship with the club that he's reporting on, although he accepts that there are certain boundaries in operation that he would be naïve to cross. He's aware, after all, that he's in a privileged, responsible position (that he admits to relishing) in being able to provide key information to fans via the various media outlets that his company utilises. Furthermore, he appreciates that what he writes is there for scrutiny and reference for evermore – the most memorable stage for him being the momentous 2-0 Championship Play-Off Final victory over Middlesbrough at Wembley Stadium on that gloriously sunny afternoon on the 25th of May 2015.

There are negatives in reporting on Norwich City, but these are in keeping with those experienced by thousands of supporters during a season concerning the distance of travel, delays, diversions and inadequate links to motorways. These are all well-known hindrances and, as the city is not moving anywhere geographically anytime soon, will always be a persistent spoke in the wheel.

It's not that the match-day coverage aspect always goes without a hitch either. During the game at Spurs on the 5th of December 2021, on what was an exceptionally cold afternoon, Paddy was alarmed to find his laptop had developed a fault down the left-hand side of the keyboard rendering it partly inoperable, although somehow he found a way to continue. The problem got worse the following week at the Manchester United match when it totally stopped working, but fortunately, his colleague Dave Freezer was able to come to the rescue with Paddy temporarily being able to use his machine and, thankfully, complete his report.

This 'winter break' coincided with the closure of the January transfer window, but there wasn't a great deal emanating from the Carrow Road hierarchy other than a few announcements reporting fringe players who were swapping loan clubs. The 'national' press, meanwhile, apparently desperate to fill their own column inches, continued to regurgitate rumours surrounding City midfielder Todd Cantwell, aka the 'Dereham Deco' – affectionately named so by fans after a combination of his hometown near Norwich and the Brazilian-born superstar who enjoyed a glittering career with (amongst others) Porto, Barcelona and Chelsea.

We may all be excused for shaking our heads and wondering 'what on earth's happened to Todd' recently. It's not that long ago that he was looking like a star in the making, constantly being linked with moves to some of the richest teams in the land. For example, on the 3rd of January 2020, Daniel Murphy of the Manchester Evening News conveyed 'Manchester United and Man City in Todd Cantwell race'. Even at the commencement of the current season (the 17th of August 2021), he was still being touted with a big move away from Norfolk as Hannah Pinnock of the Liverpool Echo reported 'Todd Cantwell, 23, is a product of Norwich's academy and has earned plenty of admirers at Premier League clubs. Aston Villa is among the clubs most heavily linked with a move for the attacking midfielder, whilst Leeds and Leicester City have also been credited with interest. Plenty of Liverpool fans were impressed with the player's performance against the Reds in their opening game of the 2021/22 Premier League season, and Jurgen Klopp is rumoured to be an 'admirer' of the player'.

So, with all these clubs touted to be interested, plus new cash-rich-kid-on-the-block Newcastle United also sniffing about, he ended up at…Bournemouth, of the Championship, on loan for the remainder of the season at the south coast club. Let's face it, based on the quality of his spasmodic performances of late (and his general lack of availability), he'd done marvellous to get a move anywhere. Speaking to the Bournemouth website after the deal had gone through, Cantwell stated that he hoped to 'kick-start' his career with Scott Parker's team and help them return to the Premier League. He confirmed it was something that he had wanted to do, he had wanted to 'get out' and that it had been a pretty easy option for him.

City's first game without Cantwell at the club was another underwhelming FA Cup tie away from home, this time with Wolverhampton Wanderers the opposition. I wonder, when the draw was announced, if any Norwich fan actually said, 'Great! Let's go for a lovely day out at Molineux!' No? Me neither. Nevertheless, the away faithful were treated to yet another 1-0 victory to put their team in the hat for the heady heights of the 5th round. Kenny McLean was the unlikely match-winner, looping in a back header from an inswinging Billy Gilmour free-kick – it was great to see this type of positive impact from the Scot rather than the negative finger-pointing bollocker of teammates version that we have become accustomed to. Next round? Liverpool (away, of course).

A couple of days after the Molineux date, it was time to return to Carrow Road for the return fixture against Crystal Palace, just six weeks after the 0-3 defeat. It was also time for my seasonal debut in the Adam & Eve, the legendary, historic, oldest public house in Norwich that dates back to 1249. Let's just dwell on that fact for a moment...people have been quenching their thirsts here for an incredible 773 years, with the first customers being the workmen who were building the nearby cathedral. Set in a former monastic brewery, the monks who owned the building appear to have been a generous bunch (or should that be Order) as they also gave ale to the patients of the equally historic Great Hospital (also founded in 1249) that the pub backs onto, purely for medicinal purposes of course.

Snuggled away on Bishopgate, equidistant between the Wig & Pen and the Red Lion, it's slightly off the beaten track (some would say secluded), and yet it was prominent enough to witness bitter battles during Kett's Rebellion in 1549 when an army of insurgents briefly took the city. The revolt was against the enclosure of common land by wealthy landowners and yeoman farmers who, not satisfied with their own vast swathes of land, greedily decided that they were also going to take the small communal plots used by peasants to graze their own animals. Robert Kett, himself a farmer, was sympathetic to the rebels' cause and gallantly became their leader.

Just across the road from the pub, inserted into the flint wall surrounding the cathedral grounds, is a plaque with the chilling words '*Near this place was killed Lord Sheffield in Kett's Rebellion the 1st of August 1549*'. The website 'Norwich360' explains that skirmishes broke out in Bishopgate between the rebels and a team of cavalry led by Sheffield. After falling from his horse and recognising that he would be captured or killed, he removed his helmet as a sign of surrender. Unfortunately for him, a rebel, who was a butcher by trade, failed to acknowledge the gesture and killed him with a blow to the head with a meat cleaver. He was carried the short distance to the Adam & Eve but was not to survive – and he is still reputed to haunt the building, running his fingers through people's hair or giving them a tap on the shoulder.

In fact, you're never short of company of the spooky variety in this hostelry as other reported 'presences' include a number of French-speaking medieval monks who lived and worked here. There's also an unnerving tale about a young boy hysterically running around the pub – his mother couldn't calm him down, and he only stopped in order to talk to a man at the bar. The thing was, only the boy could see this 'mysterious man'…

You'd never be aware of the macabre occurrences of the interior as you view the outside of the picturesque, cheery premises often bedecked with colourful, award-winning floral displays. Also to admire is the much-photographed, iconic Dutch gable end believed to have been tastefully added during a 15th-century renovation. Cheery landlady Rita McCluskey obviously likes it here (evidently unruffled by the phantom behaviour) as she's recently celebrated twenty-one years at the helm.

As I pop into the Adam & Eve a couple of hours before the game, I'm hoping to attract some ethereal inspiration from the 'locals' to enable me to complete the cryptic crossword in the Norwich Evening News. Nothing's happening though; I'm not getting any vibes. I've only filled one in so far, and that's two across. What was the clue Neil, I hear you ask? Well, here you are…**2A: Postman drops bag**. But how many letters are there Neil, I hear you ask? **Answer: Blumming hundreds of 'em!!!** Haha!

Although the crossword remains unsolved, it's been a successful evening for me so far as I rather cleverly remembered not to bang my head when entering the pub.

I'm not overly tall, but I can be overly stupid and I never seem to learn from several painful lessons regarding the low entrance here. On the approach, I tell myself, "I must remember the low roof, I must remember the low roof" then THWONK!…you can imagine me sitting there in a dishevelled heap with cartoon-style imaginary birds fluttering around my bonce. Still, I've got in OK tonight, so all's good so far.

The pub undoubtedly benefits from the abundance of historical niceties and is an understandable magnet for tourists seeking well-kept ale and home-cooked food. Also profiting from having an atmospheric interior with its low oak beams, nooks and crannies, steps aplenty and doors on latches, it was reported to be the last hostelry in Norwich to serve 'beer from the wood' back in the early 1970s – this is quite easy to visualise even today when sat in the main bar area.

After a couple of decent pints of Adnams Southwold Bitter (and no spookies encountered), it was time to move onwards. "I must remember the low roof, I must remember the low roof" I continued to repeat the mantra to myself (while also taking note of the 'Please Mind Your Head' sign above the door), keen to complete a momentous double of not banging my head on the way in OR out. "Thanks for your custom. Have a good night," beamed the barman, momentarily distracting me. THWONK!

By the kickoff time of 19:45, I'm happy to report I'd fully regained my faculties, and it was a good job I had as Teemu Pukki put the Canaries ahead after just 38 seconds, sending Carrow Road wild in the process. It was the fastest goal by any team in the top flight so far this season. He had another couple of chances before half- time that could have put the game out of the visitor's reach, but a combination of hesitancy and vigilant defending meant the score remained 1-0 at the break.

Palace's enigmatic, mercurial striker Wilfrid Zaha then took centre-stage, returning to the side after featuring for the Ivory Coast in the recent African Cup of Nations. Before the game started, his club manager Patrick Vierra, had questioned his ability to be consistent in his performances and how predictive this was to be within the space of a few second-half minutes. Firstly, we witnessed a majestic strike from him that would have beaten any goalkeeper in the world, curving a beautiful twenty-yard effort from the corner of the 18-yard box over and beyond a full-stretch Angus Gunn for the equaliser. However, within no time at all, we'd gone from appreciating the sublime to having a good old chuckle at the frankly ridiculous.

As City defender Max Aarons clipped the heel of the onrushing Tyrick Mitchell, it was no surprise to anyone when the referee, Paul Tierney, awarded a spot-kick to Palace. Zaha, still 'buzzing' after his wonder strike, nonchalantly stepped up to take it, slipped then scuffed his kick several feet wide of Gunn's right-hand post for the worst penalty since Diana Ross's spectacularly bad effort at the 1994 World Cup Finals opening ceremony in Chicago's Soldier Field (witnessed by a live crowd of 67,000 that included newly elected President Bill Clinton in an event hosted by Oprah – we should have known what was about to happen when the talk-show hostess fell off the stage immediately after introducing the songstress-turned-penalty-fluffer). To be fair to Diana Ross, she was wearing the tallest pair of stilettos, whereas Zaha had unsurprisingly plumped for the traditional football boot.

The following day the Norwich Evening News revelled in the miss, with a front-page photo of Zaha's left leg slipping away as he struck the ball, with the headline 'Zaha-ha-ha!' and a subtitle body blow of 'Penalty miss hands City point'.

Before the game, Dean Smith had spoken about the strangeness of momentum, with nobody really knowing what it is and where it comes from, and that you can definitely feel it whether it's for or against you. He also mentioned that his players were becoming more streetwise (the official term for shithouse), thus adding a crucial new level to what is required to compete and win games in the Premier League. He did not say if he thought the two were linked, but it was surely more than just a coincidence that his team's fortunes had improved in recent weeks. It was definitely positive momentum that Norwich City were currently enjoying, and long may it continue as, with moneybags Manchester City on the immediate horizon, such belief can be snatched away at very short notice - this league is absolutely brutal.

The point against Crystal Palace wasn't enough to see the Canaries climb back out of the bottom three (they'd dropped back in the previous evening after Newcastle's victory over Everton) but come the end of the season, who knows how crucial it could be for the club's safety aspirations.

CHAPTER 13
MANCHESTER CITY (H)
12TH FEBRUARY 2022

"It's not all about the money – just ask United!" said the cock-a-hoop Liam Gallagher lookalike strutting up King Street after the game, in response to a Norwich fan who was publicly bemoaning the colossal financial gulf between his team and the 'Citizens' of Manchester. I assumed it was 'underperforming' cross-city rivals Manchester United (currently 5th in the league and through to the last 16 of the Champions League, let's remind ourselves) he was referring to; after all, there are plenty of other Uniteds in the football pyramid including Southend, Colchester, Cambridge or Peterborough for example. Let's face it though, it would be astonishing for a fan of one of the UK's 'elite' to make reference to a club outside of the Premier League – do they actually acknowledge that a domestic football life exists anymore outside the top tier?

Manchester City supporters certainly should do as previously in 1997-98, their team plummeted into the old Third Division containing players such as Gerry Creaney,

Tony Vaughan and Barry Conlon. It was a totally different story (and more of a level playing field) back then. The following season, after home and away 1-1 draws with Chesterfield and a selection of 2-1 defeats against divisional heavyweights Lincoln City, York City and Oldham Athletic, they stumbled into the playoffs (which they eventually won, beating Gillingham in an epic encounter) after finishing an overall third behind Fulham and Walsall.

There are no Creaneys, Vaughans or Conlons in the current squad. At his disposal, manager Pep Guardiola has some of the best footballers in the world, signed for eye-watering amounts. Let's have a look at the eleven players (and associated ballpark transfer fees) that he selected for today's game:

- Ederson **£35m** / Walker **£45m** / Ruben Dias **£57m** / Ake **£41m** / Bernardo **£43m** / Fernandinho **£34m** / Gundogan **£21m** / Mahrez **£60m** / Sterling **£49m** / Zinchenko **£1.7m** / Foden **£0** (Academy) – that's just shy of **£400m** in total.

Also worth noting are substitutes De Bruyne **£54m** and Stones **£50m** while Grealish **£100m** was not in the squad due to injury…and I'm only skimming the surface regarding total squad spend.

Surprisingly, considering the club's vast wealth, they don't always have things their own way. The fly in the ointment tends to be when one of their own players is approaching the latter part of his contract and is considering his available 'options' (i.e. he's after some more dollar). On the eve of the game, Dave Anderson of The Mirror reported that the latest dilemma related to the future of Riyad Mahrez. Manchester City was attempting the near-impossible feat of preserving some semblance of their current wage structure with his reported **£120,000** a week contract due to expire in 16 weeks time. He will be 32 then, and they will have to decide whether to hand him another six-figure agreement or not. Apparently, he would want at least another two years on his contract, which could add up to a **£12m** commitment.

I make no apology for making the opening of this chapter appear as if you've mistakenly dipped into a column from the Financial Times, but it really IS 'all about the money', isn't it?

Here's something else that we shouldn't forget. The European Super League (nauseating motto: 'The best clubs. The best players. Every week.') was a proposed seasonal club competition that would have been initially contested by 20 clubs. Announced in April 2021, it met with serious community condemnation from all and sundry in England, with much of the criticism surrounding elitism and the lack of competitiveness – it would have consisted of only the biggest/richest teams on the continent with no promotion into or relegation out of. You just needed clout and wonga, basically. Public backlash ensured that the six Premier League clubs withdrew (a decision I was very disappointed with as I had hoped they would all skedaddle and leave the rest of us in peace). Manchester City and Manchester United would have been founder members.

Out of the initial twelve clubs that had signed up to be involved, all were included in the 2021 Forbes list of the most valuable football clubs. It had been hoped by the creators that the competition would 'provide higher quality matches and additional financial resources.' I re-iterate it really IS 'all about the money'.

I'm not saying that it's impossible for Norwich to beat Manchester City these days. After all, we disposed of them rather nicely in September 2019 with that 3-2 victory. It is still eleven human beings versus eleven human beings. It's just that to beat them, all the yellow and green ducks need to be in a row, the players need to perform at the absolute summit of their game (working extremely hard while showing exceptional quality on the ball), showing no fear, benefitting from huge slices of luck with a capable, consistent referee (and unfortunately today the 'man in the middle' was to be the lumbering, expressionless Andre Marriner). On the other hand, Guardiola's superstars need to collectively have an off day.

The scheduled kickoff time for the game was 17:30. I must confess that, for me, this is probably the most awkward of times as I appear to be incapable of planning a suitable pre-match routine that doesn't end with me facing the prospect of not being allowed entry to the ground due to my pro-active alcohol intake.

Three o'clock kick offs?...no problem. I'm eagerly out of the traps at 11, start drinking on the outskirts of the city centre, followed by a steady walk in the general direction of Carrow Road, maybe calling at a couple of other decent establishments along the way. Effectively, I'm on real ale auto-pilot. I know where I want to go, I know where I don't want to go, and I get the feeling that a high percentage of my fellow Norwich fans are of the same ilk. It's comfortable, manageable, doable and enjoyable.

If it's a half past five kick off, I find my day anxiously chaotic. I'm still awake at the same time, I still want to eat at roughly the same time, and I still want to be 'out and about' at the same time. Should I have a lie-in, should I delay breakfast and lunch, should I hang fire, do a few errands, even do a bit of shopping? Nah, sod that it's match-day! But once I'm out, the doubts start to creep in. Have I actually come out too early, should I drink at a slower pace, do I need to be drinking a lower strength beer than usual and have I factored in that I need to eat more strategically?

Today's pre-match company is provided by the delectable Denise. Life and soul Paul was entertaining a couple of Manchester City supporting ex-work colleagues, proud Yorkshireman Wiggy was on the sick list, while Sheffield-based Richard was on his way to the Fine City but not expecting to arrive until just before the start of the game.

It can definitely be classed as an alternative type of pre-match session with Denise. There's no doubt that she's engaging company, and there's not a chance that the conversation will ever hit a lull. It's just that instead of typical, well-worn discussions with Paul, Wiggy and Richard regarding the merits of a 4-4-2 formation with Idah pushed up top to give Pukki a hand or, the excellent balance of hops, fruit and barley in Woodforde's Nelson Revenge or, the benefits of wearing a suitable pair of properly fitting running shoes to aid performance in a half marathon, we have an entirely different level of chat. This can include highlighting what important jobs need doing in the garden once the weather improves (and subsequently which ones require attention first) or, is it the right time for the lounge to be decorated (and if so, in what colours) or, have I heard the new album by James Morrison (and if not, do I want to). I'm slightly out of my comfort zone, and yet it's all good productive stuff. It can definitely be taxing, and, like my team, I do need to be 'On The Ball', of course. I am thankful for her company though.

This afternoon I have taken her to the Coachmakers Arms, a distinctive looking three-storey building situated in an unprepossessing location towards the City end of the rather busy St Stephens Road. An old 17th-century coaching inn, the Norfolk Pubs website contains details of licensees going back as far as 1747. Inside, there's nothing outstanding; it's just a nice, comfortable pub that offers a good selection of half a dozen or so locally sourced ales that are snuggled behind the bar on stillage, with the firkins cosily wrapped in lagging as though they are ready for a good night's sleep. Again, as with most premises dating back this far (plus the captivating fact that this one stands on the site of a former asylum), there are rumours of ghostly activity that all add to the general atmosphere. Immediately beyond the back door, there's a spacious courtyard drinking area plus a pleasant patio.

It's outside the front of the Coachmakers that I really want Denise to see today. Why's that Neil, I hear you ask? Well, thanks for inquiring. To the right-hand side of the pub's main façade (proudly and prominently positioned above and to the right of the entrance to what would have been the stables, back in the day) lays a most wonderful 3D mural created by genius sculptor John Moray-Smith. Depicting a street scene in front of the splendid St Stephens Gates (based on an engraving by Henry Ninham 1793-1874) this is an exquisite, detailed piece of art that is there for us all to see, whenever we want, free of charge.

In an early example of branding, local brewery Morgans commissioned Moray-Smith in the 1930s to create original murals of local relevance to decorate their pubs. Many articles have been written about him over the years and yet, other than a unanimous agreement that he was eccentric, there is not too much definite information on the man. He was deemed to be a mysterious figure, never known to have posed for a photograph with the only image of him being one drawn by a neighbour.

Regarding the eccentricity, there are marvellous memories from locals seeing him work on this (and other) murals across Norwich, putting a leg over a pole and hanging his paint pot over his foot whilst wearing jodhpurs and bright red shoes. I would have paid to see that spectacle.

"That's really brilliant. It's very detailed and actually quite beautiful, crammed full of life and vibrancy, animation and colour," said the clearly impressed delectable Denise, as we stood admiring the mural from across the road. "I wonder how much it's worth?" See, it's always about the money…

I'm pleased to announce that I was allowed entry into the ground without a challenge – my attempt at 'pacing' my drinking was thus classed as being successful. Norwich had a real go at Manchester City early on as well, where a Pukki effort was well saved by Ederson, followed by a Hanley header that smacked against the foot of the post (and then away from danger) moments later. The Citizens created chances of their own, the most notable being a left-footed in-swinger from Bernardo that also hit the woodwork before conveniently bouncing into the grateful hands of Norwich custodian Gunn.

However, the writing was very clearly on the wall for the Canaries after half an hour as Raheem Stirling curled in the opener with a strike very similar to that of Zaha's three days prior. The game was effectively over a few minutes after halftime as a scrappy, scrambled effort from Phil Foden was adjudged to have crossed the line, despite the valiant attempts of Hanley. It was then damage limitation time for the home team, who were resigned to chasing shadows for the remaining 40 minutes. The supremely confident Manchester outfit played their own cruel (albeit mind-numbingly tedious) version of keep-ball, before scoring a further two goals, as Sterling completed his hat-trick, to run out 4-0 victors. Belief had collectively drained out of both team and supporters with the award of that second goal.

I must admit that the second half sapped the life out of me. At one stage, I genuinely thought that the game was approaching the full-time whistle, only to glance at the stadium clock to my right that informed me 63 minutes had gone, with still approximately half an hour still to go. At first, I thought there must be a fault with it and that it must have stopped; a quick scan of my own timepiece disappointingly confirmed this was not the case.

The result kept the Canaries in the relegation zone, one point and one position from safety, while Manchester City went 12 points clear of second-placed Liverpool (Norwich's next opponents) with this, their 14th victory out of the last 15 Premier League games. The 0-4 defeat would not be regarded as a season-defining loss, just like the 3-2 victory over the same team a couple of years back had not been classed as a season-defining victory, followed by a winning run of results concluding in Premier League survival.

After the game, in an interview with the BBC's Jonathan Pearce, an unusually arrogant Pep Guardiola boasted that "it looks easy to play like this, but it's very difficult." It appeared to have escaped his attention that, with the obscene embarrassment of riches that he has at his disposal, he should have a better chance of coaching the players to effectively play that way than most other managers, not only in the Premier League but in world football. I wonder if he would be as accomplished if he worked under the same financial restraints as, let's say, Chesterfield, Lincoln City, York City and Oldham Athletic. I guess we'll never know as we're all now well aware, it really IS 'all about the money'.

CHAPTER 14

BRENTFORD (H)

5TH MARCH 2022

Southampton v Norwich City, Friday night 20:00 kickoff. Live…on Sky Sports. You utter bell-ends #1.

When selecting this game for live coverage, there could not have been one thought from the 'satellite pay TV company' planners for the travelling fan. From Norwich, it's a 400-mile (plus) round trip to Southampton's St Mary's Stadium where, on the outward journey specifically, City fans could be vying for lane space on the M25 London Orbital with the capital's commuters – all desperately trying to get home for the weekend. It's a similarly distanced journey from my Chesterfield base as well, although my route goes in a straight line down the centre of the country, just as though it's been precisely cut by a talented surgeon with his trusty scalpel.

Let's have a look at the return journey to Norwich after the game if public transport is your preferred mode of travel. Well, if you wanted to channel your inner Mo Farah and run it to Southampton Central railway station (you're telling me you don't?...me neither), you could just about catch the 22:21 Southern Railway service to Havant. There would then be a wait of 36 minutes before hopping on a South Western train to Guildford, where you would then have to endure a bleak middle of the night interval of 3 hours and 48 minutes before another South Western service takes you onwards to London Waterloo. A transfer to London Liverpool Street would enable you to hook onto good old Greater Anglia's 06:30 early morning offering, hitting the Fine City 1 hour and 50 minutes later at 08:20. If you were totally off your rocker, and you would have to be to even contemplate it, this journey would take you 9 hours and 59 minutes – oh yeah, and for the privilege, you would have had to fork out £90.80 for the cheapest standard single fare. There would not be a shadow of a doubt that the rest of the weekend would be a fatigue-induced write-off as well.

As I said, utter bell-ends.

For much of the game, it was painful viewing as the Saints of Southampton handed out what was tantamount to a 0-2 battering that comically featured a Keystone Cops-style opening goal. Firstly, City's Brandon Williams inadvertently gifted the ball back to a threatening Livramento (after initially winning the tackle), who then dangerously crossed low into the six-yard box. Next, Angus Gunn spontaneously stuck out his right boot to make contact with the cross only to deflect it against the covering Max Aarons and straight into the path of opposition striker Adams who was stood on the goal line. He, in turn, made an absolute mess of his first free swipe at an empty goal, falling over in the process, before eventually managing to scoop the ball over a despairing Aarons and into the net from a prone position. The scorer then jumped up and sprinted off jubilantly towards the nearest corner flag (as they do), complete with 10-yard knee slide (as they do) as though he had just belted a twenty-yard volley into the top corner (as they do). At this stage, all we were missing were bulbous red noses for the Norwich defenders who (as they forlornly looked on) would also collectively be holding bouquets of drooping plastic flowers. Meanwhile, referee Simon Hooper would be heading back towards the centre circle on a trick circus unicycle (obviously with a traditional wonky wheel) whilst honking away on a retro clown horn in order to confirm the goal. Honk! Honk! Honk! Honk!

On 88 minutes, we did get to see that twenty-yard screamer, courtesy of the right boot of Southampton's Oriol Romeu, which finally sealed the win for the home team. Overall, it had been a dishearteningly abject performance from the Canaries and, a short while after the full-time whistle had blown, a desolate Dean Smith admitted, "The better team won on the night; we can't argue with that. If we only have six or seven out of ten performances, we won't win games in the Premier League."

With his team rooted again to the bottom of the league and five points from safety, he'd not managed, so far anyway, to have the meteoric effect that Stuart Webber (and everybody else concerned with the club, for that matter) would have hoped for. Agreed, he had overseen a couple of good spells, but with twelve games remaining the situation was now desperate.

Do you know what though? He'd only got the same parts, the same components at his disposal as his predecessor Daniel Farke (remember, there had not been any new additions during the January transfer window). He could tinker about with them all he wanted, but, as with a car with the same basic mechanisms, it is impossible to transform the standard family saloon into a turbo-charged limo. All you can effectively expect to achieve is to stick on some 'go-faster stripes'.

Interestingly, Norwich had received plaudits for their 'plucky, resilient' performance at Liverpool FC just six days before the Friday night rendezvous on the south coast. They had been under the cosh (some would say 'riding their luck') for most of the first half before Milot Rashica stunned the majority of the Anfield crowd by giving his team a totally unexpected lead with his first league goal, a deflected strike wrong-footing Alisson before nestling inside the keeper's left-hand post in the 48th minute.

The shock result was unquestionably on, that was until the much-vaunted attacking trio of Mane, Salah (with his 150th goal for Liverpool in just 233 appearances), and Diaz decided to make their mark in the last 30 minutes to give The Reds a 3-1 victory. Considering the overwhelming intensity and passion of a Premier League game featuring 22 ultra-professional players, it was bewildering how much room the three strikers had been permitted by the City defenders when scoring their goals. They would not have expected to benefit from any greater amount of yardage if they had been one of Antony Gormley's 'Another Place' spectacular (and yet haunting) sculptures on nearby Crosby beach.

And we were back on Merseyside less than two weeks later for the fifth round of the FA Cup...

Liverpool v Norwich City, Wednesday night 20:15 kickoff. Live…on ITV. You utter bell-ends #2.

The Liverpool Echo displayed the headline 'Smith hits out at late kickoff for FA Cup clash' in reference to the City boss's acknowledgement that "Certainly it is too late for the away fans to travel and to be expected to travel back." It was, of course, a very valid point, but at least the commitment of the Norwich fans was rewarded by their club, who arranged free coach travel for the six-hour cross country journey to the north-west (reports were that the coaches left Carrow Road at 13:00 and limped up outside Anfield at 19:00).

If the re-scheduling by Sky of the Southampton game had caused consternation among the green and yellow network, this decision, by ITV for a midweek game let's remind ourselves, was deemed to be even more heartless. However, I think I have a solution that would result in this type of scheduling being a thing of the past…

I propose that 'The Planner' responsible for the timing of the fixture should have been forced to travel on one of the Club Canary coaches. For the journey, he would be strapped into a window seat next to an individual who, for argument's sake, has a total disregard for personal hygiene (and we perhaps would all concede that there would have been at least one of said individuals travelling to Anfield). The bus 'companion' would have a full day's supply of sardine and horseradish sandwiches with accompaniments of savoury eggs and cheesy wotsits. Ideally, the topics of conversation should be limited to traffic jams, roadworks, the weather, medical issues, and politics, plus an in-depth analysis of why the acquaintance had voted for Brexit or

Remain. Condensation would be freely running down the windows, the air conditioning is on the blink and the driver's got the radio on, but it's not exactly on the right frequency. Meanwhile, the chap in the seat behind is rather enjoying himself by casually off-loading gaseous elements built up as a result of his full breakfast and a couple of pints that he's hurriedly just quaffed in the Queen of Iceni on Riverside. Six hours of that there and back? I think we'd find all games would revert to a Saturday afternoon with a 3 o'clock start.

As I said, utter bell-ends.

I was looking forward to arriving in Liverpool more than usual as I was meeting up with my youngest daughter Alisha, who resides in the city. Always delightful and charming company, she was waiting for me on the platform as my East Midlands Railway carriage tentatively crept through the suburbs and then into Lime Street station. On arrival, she had a surprise in store for me. "Dad, before the game, I'm taking you to the Walker Art Gallery. You'll love it!"

"Excellent!" I enthusiastically replied before enquiring, "I assume this is a singularly named hipster beer emporium new to the Liverpool scene that I am thus far unaware of?"

"Errr no, Dad – it actually is an art gallery." Culture and Neil Collings in the same sentence on a match day; hey, who'd have thought it.

So five minutes later, there I was, all eager and ready for a pint, perusing beautiful paintings, sculptures and decorative arts, all housed in a most impressive building built over 130 years ago. And do you know what, it was really enjoyable. As someone whose most impressive contribution to the art world was the drawing of a penis on a filthy works van many years ago, I found some of the paintings incredible. But what was your favourite Neil, I hear you ask? Well, thanks for inquiring. The one that really caught my (our) eye was titled 'One of the Family' and painted by Frederick George Cotman in 1880. A romantic, heart-warming scene of rustic domestic life, it fundamentally shows a farmer returning home after a hard shift on the land for his meal. As you can imagine, there's a lot going on in the scene, focused around the family dining table. For example, there's a loving grandma slicing a loaf of crusty bread; there's a sheepdog optimistically peering at the farmer's wife for a titbit, there's at least one of the three children ravenously getting 'stuck into' his dinner while in the middle of the table rests a steaming (meat and potato?) pie that certainly made me want a piece. Meanwhile, the farmer is stood adoringly looking at his family from the darkened corner of the room while his horse inquisitively looks on at the scene through the top part of the stable-type door. So who's the 'One' that the painting's title refers to? Sorry, I can't tell you! You'll just have to visit the gallery and have a look for yourself...

The Liverpool Echo (other than reporting on Dean Smith's thoughts on the late kickoff time) was also mulling over the chances of The Reds winning an unprecedented quadruple – can you imagine that? At a time when Norwich are struggling to win one game, they are contemplating the prospects of winning all four trophies that they are competing in: Carabao Cup (which they had already won the previous Sunday for a record ninth time), Premier League, Champions League and FA Cup.

By the end of the 90 minutes, they had improved their chances of at least achieving success in the latter competition after a 2-1 victory secured their place in the quarter-final draw. Once again, Takumi Minamino was City's nemesis, the Japanese international netting both goals to add to the double he'd notched at Carrow Road back in September. It was not as straightforward a win for Liverpool as it appeared it would be at halftime (with the score at 2-0), with Norwich showing some fight late on with a Lukas Rupp strike reducing arrears on 76 minutes. Afterwards, goalkeeper Alisson had to be alert to push a Jon Rowe shot over the bar to safety to ensure the hosts held on to secure their passage into the last eight. The final result also meant that Liverpool had now beaten Norwich for the fourth time this season – the first time in their history that they had beaten the same team four times in a single campaign.

For the record, the coaches transporting the Norwich fans back through the night to Norfolk pulled up outside the Carrow Road stadium at 04:55. Sardine and horseradish sarnies, anyone?

Just three days later, we were all back in Norwich for a crunch game against fellow relegation strugglers Brentford. Some City fans were classing the game as 'must win'; others were pitching it as 'must not lose', while it appeared that the remainder had given up the survival ghost quite a while ago.

The most important thing on my mind, as my pleasingly 'on time' EMR train arrived at Thorpe station at 11:13, was where to go for some food – after the 3 hours and 29 minutes journey (with no onboard catering), I was ravenous. Life and soul Paul was again out and about with a couple of ex-work colleagues and not going to the game, proud Yorkshireman Wiggy was still on the sick list, while Sheffield-based Richard was on his way to Tenerife for some warm weather, rest and relaxation. The world was my oyster, therefore as, with no pre-arranged route to adhere to, I could go where I wanted.

The Coach and Horses, just around the back of the station, seemed like a splendid idea as they always have a decent selection of hearty 'match day food' to choose from. So, five minutes after exiting through the station ticket barriers, I keenly entered an already buzzing pub, ordered a pint of CHB Dreadnought and took a seat with menu in hand.

As predicted, I quickly decided on chilli and chips (of course I did, I always do in here) and made my way back to the bar. "Can I order some food, please" I asked expectantly, only to receive the reply "Sorry mate, don't do food until 12."

Bugger - no problem though, as I had a cunning Plan B. I'd initially intended to walk up to the north of the city anyway and visit the Brewery Tap and Duke of Wellington as it had been a while since I had frequented these two fine drinking establishments; and there were a couple of good eating options that I could exploit on my way there. First of all, as I climbed up Silver Road, I could delightfully smell the chips that were being fried at Silver Fish Bar. "Fish, chips and peas - that'll do nicely," I thought. However, it was body blow number two as, once at the chippy, I read with dismay that it didn't open until noon, and I was ten minutes early.

Bugger – no problem though, as there was my second alternative option that I could fall back on a mere short stroll away, this being the Crusty Corner Bakery on the corner of Bell Road. Highly recommended in the area for their 'freshly baked bread and cakes, scrumptious filled rolls, pies, pastries and sausage rolls' I was just about to start salivating at the prospect of some tasty food at last when I spotted the owner switching the shop light off and disappearing through the back door – he'd closed for the weekend!

Hmmmm…was it turning out to be one of those days, I wondered?

Well, I'm pleased to report that the Brewery Tap and Duke of Wellington initially came to the rescue. A large-ish sausage roll accompanied by a pint of Fat Cat Tom Cat was devoured in the former, followed by a pint of Oakham Bishops Farewell and a bag of cheese and onion crisps in the latter. I agree that this was not turning out to be the healthiest of lunches but, then again, I never said my body was a temple.

I was definitely enjoying (and no doubt healthily benefitting) from the brisk walking between venues. My next port of call was to be the King's Head on Magdalen Street and again, it had been a while since I had taken this route. I was pleasantly surprised to see that the old, neglected Magpie public house had finally been converted into apartments; it was comforting to see the long-closed independent Turner's shoe shop was still standing ('Scissors and shears sharpened here'); it was also mind-blowing to observe that the brutalist (and derelict for more than 20 years) Sovereign House had still not been demolished. Were the authorities waiting for it to fall down of its own accord?

On arrival, the King's Head was its usual calmness personified that we have come to expect and enjoy, and yet this has not always been the case in its three hundred years history. In fact, by 2004, it's fair to say that the pub (first mentioned in dispatches as a coaching inn way back in the early 1700s) was well known for being 'rough and ready'; a place where you were more likely to get a slap in the face than you were a decent pint, a place where you wiped your feet on the way out. Basically, for want of a better phrase, it was on its arse.

However, a couple of local entrepreneurs (Roland Coomber and Jonathan Smith) saw something in the old tavern that nobody else could at the time. They purchased the freehold and set about extensively renovating it into, what was and still is, a much appreciated, friendly, social, atmospheric pub handily located in this bustling area. The initial re-opening took place in May 2005.

Unpretentious and proud of being a 'keg-free' outlet, it was keen on supporting the plethora of local breweries, with the main selling point being the 10-11 well-kept ales that were on offer. There was no music, no TV and no fruit machines – the only noise being the general chatter of contented customers pleasantly discussing their day while enjoying a pint.

Stephen George and his wife Lesley became active on the Norfolk real ale scene just a year after the pub's re-opening in 2006 when they purchased the Reedham-based Humpty Dumpty Brewery. Stephen, a native of the United States of America, had originally developed a passion for real ale after a spell living in Belgium (where he'd become a member of the CAMRA equivalent) plus a memorable visit to the Great British Beer Festival at Olympia in 2004 cemented this love affair. He'd dabbled with home brewing back in the States, then officially added to his basic and yet burgeoning skills by attending a brewing course in Cheam soon after attending the GBBF.

Content with life as a popular and successful brewer, it was on a night out around Norwich in 2013 that Stephen was alerted to the fact that Roland and Jonathan were looking to sell the King's Head. He saw himself and Lesley as being the ideal pair to buy the freehold (and not with a view to flooding the place with their own ales either), keen on maintaining what had made the pub a thriving success in the first place. He had no desire to alter anything, which was a refreshing change to the norm for a new owner...and nine years later, this is still the case today.

You can say that Stephen is definitely a 'hands-off' sort of owner as well, preferring to take a back-seat, behind-the-scenes role regarding the general running of the pub. In his own words, he's there to "pay the bills and buy the non-beer stock such as snacks and spirits." He has a couple of more than capable, dedicated lieutenants who manage the pub and who he heartily acknowledges as "mainstays" – manager Alison and cellar-man Charlie (who's as enthusiastic and passionate about beer as it is possible to be, even adding to his all-round knowledge by helping out at local breweries such as S&P and Wildcraft).

This overall approach (i.e. retaining the aspects that made the pub a success in the first place plus allowing others better placed to do the required job) has certainly paid dividends as the King's Head is proudly a two-time winner of the Norwich & District CAMRA Pub of the Year award (2017 and 2022) – no mean feat in this city of wonderful real ale institutions.

As I settled onto a pew with my old mate Daz, opposite the front bar with a pint of Green Jack Golden Best, I just had that nagging feeling that this was going to be the highlight of the day...

The game ended up being all about Brentford striker Ivan Toney and VAR on what can only be described as a totally frustrating and dreadfully disappointing afternoon for the home team and its supporters. Toney, who netted a hat-trick, smashed home the opener on 32 minutes after being the latest honorary recipient of the Antony Gormley sculpture award for the amount of space found in the Norwich penalty area.

City needed a response and nearly got one at the beginning of the second period when Williams appeared to be pushed over from behind – the referee and VAR agreed that there was no infringement. At the other end, from a Brentford corner, a high boot from Gibson was not initially spotted by the on-pitch officials. However, VAR advised the referee to have a look at his pitch-side monitor and after a quick peek, the visitors were granted a penalty that Toney duly dispatched for his second. And six minutes later, he'd claimed the match ball after confidently dispatching penalty number two after Gibson had brought him down with a clumsy challenge.

Norwich thought they'd secured a lifeline through Rashica after 67 minutes, only for VAR to intervene once more, ruling the strike out after adjudicating that Pukki had been offside in the build-up (with Brentford's Mbeumo also having one chalked off in a similar manner). By the time the Finnish international had netted a late consolation in the 3-1 defeat, many home fans had left the stadium.

After picking up some after-match train provisions from Morrisons, I re-joined the throngs heading back down Koblenz Avenue towards the railway station. It was a contrast of styles between the two tribes of supporters; crestfallen Norwich fans opting for a doleful trudge, hands in pockets and heads bowed, whereas the exuberant opposition tried out a mixture of handsprings, front pikes and cartwheels. I then entered the station and immediately read the information boards:

'This train is for SHEFFIELD. Please note this train will not stop at LANGLEY MILL, ALFRETON, CHESTERFIELD & SHEFFIELD. This train is operated by East Midlands Railways'. You utter bell-ends #3.

They ought to have included something along the lines of 'Sorry (not sorry) about this, but please be sure to keep a sane mind while attempting to jump through the many hoops that will be inconveniently lying in wait for you on your return journey. Love & Kisses. EMR'.

The Greater Anglia staff who work in the information kiosk have a tough role in situations like this. They have to provide details, as best they can, to stricken and often moody travellers heading north who want to travel on a train that is not operated by them. Nevertheless, in my experience, they do this in a seemingly empathetic manner with a smile on their face. But are they just trying to get rid of me? The lady who dealt with me advised me to catch the

21:12 Northern service to Chesterfield once I had arrived in Nottingham.

EMR had 'pulled out all the stops' for this journey in more ways than one. Once on the platform, we had a chance to view our chosen carriage. It was a pitiful-looking specimen containing two compartments that most probably dated back to the time of Dr Richard Beeching's attempts at 'reshaping' the railways of Britain back in the 1960s. To make the appearance starker, it was surrounded on the adjacent platforms by a brand, spanking new fleet of gleaming Greater Anglia rolling stock that would soon be transporting punters to Lowestoft, Sheringham and Great Yarmouth.

Once on board, and several minutes after we had departed, the situation got worse, much worse, as it soon became apparent that we would be undertaking the TWO HOURS AND FORTY-NINE MINUTES journey with no toilet facilities. On realisation, I looked longingly at my just-opened can of beer, knowing that I would be unwise to drink any of it. This train will forever be known as 'The Cross-Legged Express' – absolutely unbelievable.

The Guard, unhelpfully but maybe wisely, stayed in his compartment for the whole of the trip. The only material and advice he provided was to let us know when we had arrived at a certain destination, such as "This is March – March is your next station stop." Well, thanks a lot for that, mate. "WE KNOW WHERE WE FUCKING ARE! WE CATCH THE WRETCHED THING EVERY TWO WEEKS, FOR GOD'S SAKE." All we required was to know when we could have a wee and how best we could get home, most definitely in that order.

On arrival in Nottingham, we were notified that the previously recommended 21:12 service had been cancelled (course it was), like-wise the 23:18, meaning that the only option (other than an overnight stop on the station) was the 22:15. Furthermore, an EMR information person advised that it was unwise to catch a train over to Derby as there were no onward connections to Chesterfield that evening (I find out the following day that this had been incorrect). With no thanks to EMR, it was eventually 23:03 when I got to see the Crooked Spire again and yes, it had been 'one of those days'.

As I said, utter bell-ends.

CHAPTER 15

CHELSEA (H)

10TH MARCH 2022

Brentford's (and Ivan Toney's, for that matter) opening goal on Saturday had resulted from a well-worked and executed corner-kick routine. After the game, Dean Smith had noted, "They (Brentford) won the first flick because we were a little bit passive at the near post area. We didn't mark well enough at the far post after that." So, apart from being shite at both the front and back sticks, we're not too bad at defending corners – well, that's a relief, I can tell you. After all, it was only the eighth time this season that the Canaries had conceded from a set-piece.

On a serious note, it's mind-boggling that Norwich do not currently employ a specific, dedicated 'set piece' coach, especially as games can quite easily be won or lost in this area. There were rumours that they were considering hiring one during the summer off-season but would this not be too late? The goalkeeping coach, Ed Wootten, had apparently stepped into the breach recently (with Smith praising him for his diligent work), but this could only be classed as a stop-gap measure – his expertise is with coaching the lads with the gloves.

Alarmingly, Pink Un reporter Connor Southwell (in his match preview) identified that tonight's visitors Chelsea themselves had "a unique corner routine that sees Jorginho occupy the six-yard box before blocking the defender closest to the near post allowing a runner from a deeper position space to nod the ball into the back of the net." Well, I'm sure that with the players having received a 'flea in their ears' from the manager, plus more thorough planning from Ed Wootten, there's surely no way they'll fall for that one this evening – will they?

The morning's Pink Un also contained a scathing article from ex-City striker Iwan Roberts regarding the overall performance against Brentford. In his weekly column, he ranted, "People can whinge and moan all they want about the referee's decisions and VAR, but let's not beat about the bush: the reason Brentford beat Norwich was nothing to do with these things. Players made too many poor decisions and errors and nine times out of ten, if that happens, you lose the game."

He then continued, "There's now such a lack of belief and confidence running through the team and they need to get both back ASAP; otherwise, it's going to be good night Vienna, and back to the Championship we come." This was the issue that Chris Sutton had first warned us about back in September.

Chelsea were coming to Carrow Road as the current holders of the Club World Cup, UEFA Champions League (with £72 million striker Kai Havertz scoring the decisive goal in both of these finals) and UEFA Super Cup. In fact, the only award they had not won in Europe recently had been the Eurovision Song Contest, but I guess that's only because they've never entered it in the first place. I'm sure this could be arranged though, as they would, no doubt, just spend a fortune on a superstar singer (it'd have to be someone like Adele, Ed Sheeran or Beyonce, wouldn't it) to win it for them, if they so desired.

Or could they?

For shortly after 09:00 on the morning of the game, news emerged that sanctions had finally been placed on their owner Roman Abramovich for his links to Russian President Vladimir Putin. As a result, all his assets had been immediately frozen, with the knock-on effect for Chelsea FC being that they were now operating under a series of special restrictions. Amongst a myriad of measures, their credit cards had been suspended, they would not be allowed to sell any match tickets, there was to be no player trading, and the club shop would have to close. These were classed as extreme, chaotic circumstances with the club in apparent financial turmoil.

Abramovich had always had a commonly known ambition to make Chelsea financially stable and not solely reliable on his contributions, but that didn't appear to be the case nineteen years on from when he'd purchased them back in 2003. In fact, considering the initial panic emanating from Stamford Bridge, it looked like they were still in the same financial mess that he'd found them in. Their income streams had now been decimated, and if you do that to a club with a (rumoured) massive monthly wage bill of £28 million, then you can plummet into a fiscal abyss very, very quickly.

The government advised that they retained the right to alter or suspend the sanctions at any time and were prepared to tweak the restrictions when and where necessary in order to ensure that the Blues didn't fold – they did not intend to see a leading English team (considered by them to be a 'cultural asset') financially implode. There were many football supporters across the land who would not be shedding a single tear if this was to happen, with Chelsea acknowledged as one of the most detested clubs in England (and there are quite a few to choose from)…

As I arrived in Norwich, it appeared that Spring had finally sprung; it had been a lovely, pleasant, sunny day so far with just a slight nip to be found in the uplifting Norfolk air. I certainly had a 'spring' in my step as I made my way up through the city to the Kings Arms on Hall Road.

On arrival, the pub looked in fantastic condition, possibly benefitting from having had a lick of paint since I was last there. In the late afternoon, it was cosiness personified with the tranquil outside lanterns emitting a warm, welcoming glow. The profusion of bay windows on the front of the building gave the pub a distinctive and yet agreeably rustic appearance, while the side wall fascinatingly appears to run off at a tangent, similar to Norwich's back four when defending a corner you could say.

Classed as a 'proper local', it's been a favourite with City fans for many years. Inside, it's immaculate, well cared for and a real credit to the landlord & landlady (Stephen and Karen). Award certificates for 'Floral Display Winners' and 'Cellar Management Winners' are proudly and prominently displayed to the right of the bar. Usually rammed to the rafters on a match day, numbers can often be swelled with real ale drinking away supporters in attendance too. There were no Chelsea devotees visible today though. Eleven cask ales were advertised on the boards situated immediately above the bar, including four from the owners, Batemans Brewery (who intriguingly suggest that the pub could eventually be known as the 'Batemans Norwich Brewery Tap'). The Kings Arms also have 'probably the biggest food menu in Norwich' with Chinese, fish & chips, Indian, fried chicken, plus vegan and vegetarian options all advertised on the pub's website – but no, before you ask, they don't benefit from having what you'd assume to be probably the biggest kitchen in Norwich. They supply the plates, cutlery and condiments, leaving customers with the easy task of ordering their preferred food choice from a favourite takeaway (and there are lots of eateries to choose from that are literally yards away).

The old building is fast approaching its 200th birthday. Built in 1824, it was to be another six years before it was first licensed. Today, the Kings Arms is unnervingly quiet as I order a pint of Batemans Hooker. Is this a direct sign that Norwich fans have finally surrendered regarding the fight for Premier League survival, I wonder? A middle-aged chap walks through the door, a well-worn yellow and green bar scarf wrapped around his neck, giving off the impression that he's witnessed many games in the past. Making his way to his friends, who are comfortably sat immediately to the right of the door, he enquires, "Are we ready for tonight's thumping then, gentlemen?" and before they could answer him, he follows up with "Why oh why do we bother?" He's met with a unified collection of head shakes and shoulder shrugs that (sort of) answer him and also my initial question – and this ruthless league can do this to you. It saps you; it drains you. There's no longer any excitement or joy to be had at facing a team like Chelsea. This is die-hard territory where loyal supporters attend out of a sense of duty. I just hoped that Dean Smith's players could offer more of a fight later this evening and prove us all wrong.

It's not just the Kings Arms that's on the quiet side this evening. I walk over to the Freemasons but stop short of going through the door as I suspiciously note that there are only a couple of people stood at the bar. Maybe the pub is in the process of winding operations down, I ruminate, as I spot there is a message chalked on the outside blackboard advising that the current landlord is leaving for pastures new at the weekend.

I even walk straight to the bar and get served immediately in the Rose, which is a match-day first for me. "Thought you'd be busier than this", mentions a chap who's in the process of ordering a pizza. I select a pint of Wildcraft Wild Norfolk, a 4.2% IPA - a phenomenal beer, in my opinion. It's difficult to imagine a more tasty beer at this strength. I make a mental note that I must make a visit to the brewery in Buxton…

Meanwhile, at Carrow Road, and considering the suddenness of the sanctions placed on the visitors, it's business as usual within moments of the referee tooting his whistle to start the game. Unconditional love is a prerequisite of football fans generally, no matter what their owner has/hasn't supposed to have done or who he is/isn't alleged to be linked with. In Chelsea's case, with no English club having won more than the 21 trophies that they have since Abramovich took over the reins, the fans are never going to disrespect the oligarch. However, it still feels offensive to hear them continuously chant his name, accompanied by the sickening "We've won it all." Norwich fans retaliate with an optimistic "You've lost it all" and "Dirty Russian money."

If I told you that Chelsea were awarded an early corner, what do you think happened? Yes, you are absolutely correct – they went into a 1-0 lead after the extensively predicted near-post delivery was nodded in from a yard by Trevoh Chalobah. There were inhabitants on Tristan da Cunha who would have been aware of this set-piece routine, and yet the City defenders had not seen the e-mail, they'd not read Connor Southwell's match preview, and they'd possibly not listened to Ed Wootten. It was 2-0 after 14 minutes when Mason Mount slammed in what seemed like his 478th goal against Norwich since coming onto the scene four seasons ago while out on loan at Derby County. At this stage, a monumental hammering was on the cards.

The remainder of the first half followed a similar pattern to many we've seen recently, with a passive Norwich team collectively chasing shadows; the ever-willing Pukki running his scallops off doing his own personal beep-test between the Chelsea defenders as they nonchalantly played the cruel game of keep-ball amongst themselves. Still, there had been no further addition to the scoreline when the players retreated down the tunnel for their cuppa.

The halftime entertainment at Carrow Road has been bloody brilliant since Dean Smith became manager (bear with me on this one people), and I wholeheartedly recommend that you refrain from going down to the concourses or from moaning about City's efforts to the person next to you (this has become a very common activity in my area) and watch it. No, I'm not talking about the 'zorb balling' taking place in front of the visiting supporters in the South Stand either - for the uninitiated, this is the recognised 'official' entertainment (also known as bubble football) where two enthusiastic contestants, half encased inside inflated torus bubbles, try to score, into tiny nets, as many goals as they can against each other within a couple of minutes. I must admit, it doesn't look easy or natural, and there are the odd laughs to be had as the hapless combatants often fall over at key moments and then struggle to get back up on their feet. No, I'm definitely not talking about this activity.

The most impressive entertainment actually involves Norwich City's raft of substitutes and their manic fitness coach and is to be found in front of the Wensum area of the main stand. It commences after the time-honoured tradition of the bench warmers either expectantly trying to control 30-yard cross-field passes on their arse cheeks or sometimes trying to balance a ball on their brow for a minute as though they are performing seals – none of which you'd assume would be beneficial to them if they are later asked to enter the fray. Therefore, the 'main' activity generally takes place within the last five minutes of the interval and is well worth the wait, trust me…now let me try and explain.

The subs slowly make their way over to the touch-line - they're not in any rush as they are well aware of what is about to happen - where the fitness coach is ominously waiting. He's strategically laid out some cones in advance, and you can see he's more than ready to deliver his instructions for the forthcoming dynamic drills. He's bouncing from toe to toe and frenetically whirling his arms about as he cajoles the players to get to the cones as quickly as possible. And then he starts...he's barking out the orders, he's demonstrating (in no particular order) what looks like: sideways running with a high knee crossover step, walking lunges with rotation, linear knee raises, squats, mini sprints, fast feet, leg swings and thoracic spine rotations. He's basically throwing the 'warm-up' kitchen sink at them. They have one-second maximum to perform each drill. He randomly runs towards them aggressively (is he going to strike somebody? – I'm not sure). Then, a yard shy, he histrionically retracts as though he's strapped on the end of a giant elastic band that flirts him back to his mark. He's hyper, it's hectic and frenzied...and it's bloody hilarious. As soon as he demonstrates one exercise, he's straight onto the next. The players haven't got a chance. In truth, they hardly get close to even starting an exercise. They're bumping into each other, looking bewildered and haven't a clue what's going on. Then, as soon as it's started, it's finished. The fitness coach quickly gives them all a clap, picks up his cones, and he's off down the tunnel. The players breathe a sigh of relief. It's been breathless but great entertainment for us onlookers and well worth the admission fee.

Two of the substitutes (Lukas Rupp and Milot Rashica) had been spared these activities as they were coming on at the beginning of the second half, replacing the ineffective Mathias Normann and the out-of-sorts Christoph Zimmermann. And what an unexpected transformation we witnessed! There was a belief, intensity and bullishness about City's play that totally knocked Chelsea out of their piss-taking stride. There was even an added bonus of the boorish visiting fans falling silent, especially after the ice-cool Pukki had dispatched a 69th-minute penalty. There were lung-busting marauding runs from Max Aarons and Rashica that got fans out of their seats; there was clever, combative midfield play from Pierre Lees-Melou and Rupp while the City defence (for once) looked in total control. We nearly had an equaliser to celebrate (a header from Kenny McLean) that would no doubt have brought the house down, but ultimately it wasn't to be with that man Havertz finally putting the game to bed in injury time. Still, it had been an exhilarating second-half showing from the Canaries (why couldn't they have played like that in the opening 45 minutes?) and I, once again, had a 'spring' in my step as I made my way up Carrow Hill towards the Rose. Well, I just had to try another pint of Wildcraft Wild Norfolk, didn't I?...for quality control purposes, you must understand.

Three days later, at Leeds United's Elland Road ground, Norwich were again found wanting, after yet another abject opening 45 minutes, eventually losing the game 1-2. There had been a frenetic ending with Kenny McLean notching an equaliser for City in the 91st minute, only for Leeds to claim a winner three minutes later.

A short while after the full-time whistle had blown, Dean Smith was interviewed by the BBC. He acknowledged that his team "weren't good enough first half" and that Leeds had been the better team. He also bemoaned the fact his players "didn't have enough energy about them", and they "couldn't keep giving halves of football away." He'd had to change it again during the interval and conceded that it had been too many times that he had done this since becoming manager. When quizzed by the reporter about why this was, he confessed he didn't know why the first-half showing had been so poor and that if he did, he'd have "done something before the game as the same thing had happened against Chelsea." He accepted that there were "not an awful lot of positives" to be taken from the game, although he believed that the overall character could not be questioned. As an example, he highlighted Teemu Pukki, who was suffering with cramp towards the end and yet still managed to "make lung-busting runs down the sides of the opposition", with one of them resulting in McLean's goal after he'd fired a cross into the six-yard box.

Norwich City FC now had three weeks before their next fixture, away at Brighton, with Smith continuing "it'll be a tough three weeks" but that he aimed to productively utilise the time by working on better quality in the final third. There were "still no white flags going up, and while there are 27 points to play for, we'll still play for every one of them." As a supporter, this was heartening to hear, and it was a fact that he had pieced together a couple of mini unbeaten runs during November and January/February. However, for him to achieve his survival aims, he would now require something absolutely spectacular.

CHAPTER 16

BURNLEY (H)

10TH APRIL 2022

During the latest international break, I thought I'd check in on the City Academy and see how things had been going recently for Kenny Coker. I'd previously mentioned that he'd seemingly had a mixed start to the season, but he must have been doing something to catch the eye in the last few weeks as he had earned himself a promotion into the U23 squad. In 16 appearances for the U18s, he'd still only scored that one consolation penalty against Brighton back in September and yet, as recently as the 14th of February, had secured himself a place on the bench for the U23s game at Dartford against Charlton Athletic.

Over five weeks later, he was again an unused substitute for the U23's trip to Birmingham City's St Andrews Stadium before actually making his debut in the higher age group against Stoke City on the 25th of March, replacing Flynn Clarke in the 77th minute - a momentous occasion and another stepping stone realised in the life of a young professional footballer at Norwich City FC.

From the outside looking in, it often seems strange that match results are not of any apparent importance to the club at this level. For example, the U18s (after the 3-0 defeat to Leicester City on the 25th of March) had played twenty games with just the one victory, one draw and eighteen defeats. I sometimes ponder that the amount of defeats that the players get accustomed to at such a relatively early age can become an unfortunate habit with a losing mentality being involuntarily acquired. However, the fruitful and continuous conveyor belt of young players moving through from the different age groups into the seniors is surely proof that the operation currently being undertaken is a successful one. There will be further evidence of this in the next first-team fixture at Brighton's Amex Stadium...

For the purist, ninety minutes of Brighton v Norwich was perhaps not at the top of their weekend's footballing agenda. After all, both teams were currently on the same crushing six-game losing streak, although, in that run, the Seagulls were just pipping the Canaries in the current form table as they had a marginally better goal difference of one (-12 compared to -13). Having lost their last 4 games at the Amex, Brighton would be chasing their first home win in 3 months and attempting to score their first home goal in five matches. Nevertheless, due to the positive results achieved earlier in the season, they were still handily placed to secure the club's best-ever top tier finish – they had ended the 1981-82 season in 13th spot. I didn't foresee that we'd be hanging on to our hats during the afternoon as, taking into account Norwich's own well-known toothlessness in the goal-scoring area, the smart money was on a goalless draw.

Anyway, enough of all the pessimism! Brighton is one of my favourite away-days. It's a funky seaside city famous for being inclusive, dynamic, cosmopolitan, bohemian and possibly the only place where Sheffield-based Richard has ever been propositioned for antiperspirant by a couple of playful pole-dancers (he was carrying a rucksack at the time, so I guess it was a reasonable request).

On a beautiful, bright and cheery morning from Brighton's bustling rail station, I immediately made my way down Queens Road/West Street to the sea-front where I instantly drew in a deep breath of exhilaratingly fresh, peppery coastal air. This is what you ALWAYS do when you happen to reside in a town as landlocked as Chesterfield. It really is as though we've never seen the ocean before.

Consciously satiated by the coastal breeze, I traversed my way back through the quaint narrow lanes famous for their small and independent boutique shops and the attractively painted terraces. I was heading towards the Basketmakers Arms on Gloucester Road.

An award-winning, traditional, much-loved institution, it's reminiscent of the type of back street boozer that you may stumble upon in certain areas of London. Part of the locally operated 'Good Times' pub group, there were four beers on offer from the Fullers brewery portfolio plus a further three from Sussex-based Dark Star. But where does the pub get its name from Neil, I hear you ask? Well, thanks for inquiring. It's simply because the building is located in what was traditionally the basket-making area of Brighton.

A splendid ten minutes walk away is the Lord Nelson

Inn on Trafalgar Street. There are a few options to get there (including along what you would hope to find well-maintained residential properties on Tidy Street), and I chose to walk down Sydney Street. In a way, it's very similar to Norwich's Magdalen and St Benedict's streets with the eclectic array of shops on display, my favourite being the 'Mod' clothing outlet that still beguilingly retained the ghost signage of 'P. & A. Leach' fishmongers who had traded there sometime in the not-so-recent past.

From across the road, the Lord Nelson Inn is certainly a very photogenic hostelry with the frontage enticing you through the doors for one of their Lewes-based Harvey's Brewery 'prize Sussex ales'. Inside, it's a classic, unspoiled 'local' that's very close to the railway station and yet just far enough away from the tourist & footballing supporter tracks to retain an intimate, charming and comfortable atmosphere with none of the unwanted hustle and bustle. I found the Harvey's Armada Ale to be extremely refreshing and palatable. A 4.5% dry-hopped golden ale with a vibrant hop tone and a dry finish, as excellently described by the brewery, it's 'a port of call in any beer drinker's voyage of discovery'.

On arrival at the Amex, I found that they, too, were pleasingly dispensing Harvey's beer. This is another example of where Brighton & Hove Albion FC have got things right in so many areas since their relocation to the Falmer area back in 2011 after a long, drawn-out affair. On production of your match ticket, there's free travel to the ground on public transport within a large geographical zone, friendly and helpful stewarding, wide and spacious concourses, great uninterrupted views of the playing area and the added luxury of padded seats (although I assume, like on my latest visit, these are never utilised by visiting supporters who will always choose to stand).

In many, many ways, Brighton also impressed out on the pitch. Crisp, deft passing, lively full-backs overlapping at will, strong tackling, threatening at set-pieces, they were totally dominant. And yet somehow, unfathomably, they failed to notch the winner. They had an incredible 31 shots at goal, the most that they have ever managed in a Premier League fixture. This total included a penalty that niggly Neal Maupay (remember him?) blazed over the bar after some excellent jiggery-pokery from City stopper Tim Krul (who went face to face with the striker when he was in the act of placing the ball on the spot, warning him that he had seen his last three penalties, he'd spotted that they had all gone down the middle of the goal, and not to do that today as he would surely save it). Man of the Match Krul also made a stupendous save from a point-blank header from fellow countryman Joel Veltman in the second half.

Norwich had to defend heroically for much of a game where, in general, they lacked quality, appeared unambitious and were totally inadequate in the Brighton half. It was as though they'd had no preparation, didn't really know each other and had been thrown together out on the pitch. A contributory factor could have been the late raft of withdrawals from the squad due to injury (resulting in four Academy players - Jonathan Tomkinson, Tony Springett, Abu Kamara and Jon Rowe - being on the bench), but nonetheless, it was a very tough watch witnessing wave after wave of the home team's attacks. This was only exacerbated by a self-styled, very vocal 'expert' in the row behind me who was intent on providing a constant running commentary. So, not only was I witnessing dross I was also having to listen to it. Here are a few of his comments:

"This is fucking useless Norwich / Get a tackle in City for fuck's sake / This is a fucking shambles / Have a word Smith for fuck's sake / This is embarrassing / You haven't got a clue what you're doing / Stop pissing about with it at the back Norwich and just get rid of it / For fuck's sake stop knocking it long and play it out from the back". On and on and on and on and on he went...that is, until the exasperated chap next to me decided he needed to challenge (at least) the last two comments.

"We're all feeling it mate, but you're doing my head in. What the fuck are you on about? You're not making any sense! Knock it long/play it short. Make your mind up; what do you want!"

Luckily, for all concerned, referee Simon Hooper blew his whistle for halftime. A possible confrontation had been averted with, mercifully, the 'expert' deciding to tone it down during the second period.

I'm a big believer in the fact that no matter how bad a team is playing, they always seem to get a chance to score, and Norwich did manoeuvre a solitary chance late in the game. Talisman Pukki, latching onto a finely weighted pass from Billy Gilmour, dumped the big old lump commonly known as Lewis Dunk on his backside. Racing forward, he looked up, waiting for assistance. Substitute Jon Rowe darted to the front post expertly, taking two Brighton defenders with him leaving Milot Rashica totally unmarked on the far post. We waited with bated breath as Pukki then did his bit, expertly finding the Kosovo international...who promptly proceeded to volley the ball ten yards over the bar. Back on the halfway line skipper Hanley slumped to his knees in dismay while Normann gave out a loud cry of anguish, pulling his shirt over his head in the process.

Shall we take this opportunity to talk about Mathias Normann? I think we should. During a recent interview on Lillestrøm TV2, he made it crystal clear that if Norwich were relegated at the end of the season (which was looking more likely by the day), he would not be prepared to play in the Championship. Judging by recent performances, one can only assume that he must have aspirations to play for a team in League One (or League Two, for that matter). His current form was typified during what should have been an innocuous act at the Amex - Giannoulis took a routine bog-standard throw-in to him, no doubt expecting a bog-standard routine wall pass back in return. Normann couldn't manage that and played the ball two yards over the thrower's head. Throughout the game, he continuously failed to pass directly to a teammate. If they had all been sporting photos of a seriously large cow's arse on the front of their shirts, they would not have been in any sort of danger from being hit by Normann's out-of-tune banjo. But seriously, at any club, not just ours, why do some players (who have obviously contributed to relegation) seem to think that they are better than they are and worthy of what would ultimately be an unwarranted, unearned upwards move? I know it's just a job for them, I know it's all about the pay packet, and I'm realistic enough to know a lot of them couldn't give two hoots about Norwich City FC. But they should be more thoughtful and appreciative of fans who spend their lives traipsing up and down the country witnessing their substandard efforts. They should be more empathetic as to how fans are feeling. Personally, I see such remarks as a kick in the guts for all my fellow Canaries, both present and past (RIP my good friends Lily Kemp, Andrew Beasley and Nigel Scott). Uansett Mathias, vi sees senere og takk for ingenting, in other (Norfolk) words "sling yer uck buh".

Despite some late huffing and puffing from the home team, City somehow hung on for the 0-0 draw with the 'smart money' placed earlier in the day, proving a sound investment. As I walked down the slope outside the stadium towards nearby Falmer rail station, my thoughts drifted to the next fixture against Burnley at Carrow Road a week on Sunday. It would surely take a total transformation from what we had seen today for Dean Smith's team to get anything against their relegation rivals.

The following weekend started off in excellent fashion, with life and soul Paul picking me up in the City before kindly transporting us to the Wildcraft Brewery (owned by Mike Deal and Mark Goodman), a ten-mile drive outside Norwich on the Coltishall Road.

Back in August 2015, after the 1-1 home draw with Stoke City, Mike was sat in the Coach & Horses, Thorpe Road, with friend Mark. He had lots to talk about, and the main topic wasn't necessarily the game they'd just witnessed at Carrow Road, where Alex Neil's newly-promoted Canaries had battered the Potters but somehow failed to notch a winner. The burning issue was that he wanted to set up his own brewery after becoming disillusioned with the teaching profession. He was satisfied with the many successful home brews he'd tested at his base in Old

Costessey; all he required now was a suitable building and the necessary finances, and he'd be able to commence this new exciting chapter in his life.

Regarding the premises, Mark had a brainwave. He knew his parents owned a barn in Buxton that they weren't doing a great deal with. He would see if this could be the appropriate venue that Mike was in search of. Mike, on the other hand, decided he would go down the 'Crowdfunding' route to secure the capital needed to eventually get the venture off the ground.

I'm pleased to report that in October 2016 (after funding and premises had duly been secured and also following much hard work by Mike himself to bring the barn up to scratch) Mike produced his first-ever official brew, Wild Spice (now known as Wild Winter) for Wildcraft Brewery. Buoyed by the unanimously positive response to the new beer, he was up and running, although appreciative that much personal 'leg work' was still required to continue to promote the brewery and the future new ales that he had planned, all to his own recipes.

Six years later, things are going rather well for Wildcraft. As I mentioned in the Chelsea chapter, their beers are extremely flavoursome, with the ones that I've tried all having a much deeper, robust taste than you'd imagine from the listed ABV. In boxing terms, they'd definitely be 'punching above their weight'. I believe the (not so) secret to their success is that Mike and his team are prolific foragers in the Norfolk countryside for natural ingredients, which he tells me can include items such as nettles, raspberries and blackberries. He also mentions the much sought-after achillea millefolium, more commonly known as the yarrow flower. I've never heard of it before, but I'm gripped when he tells me the yarrow's leaves and blossoms were widely used to bitter beer before hops became popular. I'm also enthralled when I find out some of the other wonderful names that the 'yarrow' has been known by, such as nosebleed plant, old man's pepper, devil's nettle and soldier's woundwort. Great stuff!

Business continues apace for the brewery, and Mike does not see too many reasons to make wholesale changes to an already fruitful operation. However, there is a relocation on the horizon to new premises on the Worstead Farms Estate in Smallburgh, a fifteen-minute drive to the east from Buxton. Mike is particularly excited about this as he will be growing his own barley to be used in his beers, contributing to the brewery's desire to be as environmentally friendly and sustainable as possible. Plus, there will be more space available in order to hold live music events (another of his passions).

Before I'd ever spoken to Mike, I had spotted a couple of yellow and green crocheted cushions on a recent photo of the brewery (I know, I know...I should have been a detective), and so it was no surprise when Mike first confessed to being a supporter of the Canaries, holding a season ticket in the Lower Barclay for the past fifteen years. He's no different to many City fans at the moment, disgruntled with the performances and subsequent results. He was disappointed to see Daniel Farke get the push, although appreciative that a change had been required at the time. As they have continued to be rooted in the bottom three for much of the time since, Mike believes that it was the club's summer recruitment that was poor and the main cause of the substandard season so far. He goes as far as saying the team that won the Championship last season was better than the current vintage. Again, he is not alone in this view.

On our visit, Mike was at a more pressing engagement at Fakenham racecourse manning the Wildcraft marquee, leaving us in the more than capable hands of knowledgeable employee Ben. I could have stayed at the brewery all day, chatting to him and Paul, enjoying the peaceful, idyllic surroundings with young goats' kidding' around in an adjacent field. The sun was shining, and I was rather enjoying a few pints of Wild Hopster, a 5% IPA just perfect for such a lovely morning. It was going to be a good weekend; I could feel it in my relaxed bones...

For most fans, it's been hard work watching Norwich for much of this season, but there's still plenty of time for the team to get us back onside. Just one last hurrah in the Premier League before we're here again someday, showing us some fight, showing us some passion, showing us that they care. However, Burnley FC are traditionally not the easiest of opponents to get back on track against. For a while now, they've had the monopoly on the signings of big old lumps (I wondered if they have ever had their eye on Lewis Dunk), and if they changed their name to Big Lump FC everyone would instantly know which team this referred to. This policy has certainly worked well for them in the last few years; they're extremely well organised with a penchant for arrowing crosses into the box – corners, free-kicks or from open play, wallop the ball into the area and they'll gleefully attack it. And as City have acquired a reputation for collectively nodding off when aerially challenged this season, it would have to be all hands to the pump for Grant Hanley and his men to overcome this stern challenge.

But do you know what? Against all odds, Norwich were excellent throughout the whole game, courageous and vigilant in defence, combative and creative in midfield, spontaneous and clinical in attack while the Canary faithful defiantly sang, cheered and shouted encouragement. It had been a while.

Pierre Lees-Melou opened the scoring, the rangy midfielder side-footing the ball home from the edge of the box after nine minutes. City and their fans now had something to hold onto, something to defend. We have become accustomed to the consistency shown by stalwarts such as Hanley and Pukki, but it was splendid to see terrific displays from Kenny McLean with easily his best barnstorming performance this season and Mathias Normann reminding both us and any potential suitors what he is actually capable of.

Burnley did have their moments, especially just after the hour mark when sub Dwight McNeil expertly picked out Maxwel Cornet steaming in on the far post. But with the goal at his mercy, he somehow failed to hit the target, sparking howls of derision from a baying Barclay End. It was therefore left to Pukki to settle any late Norwich jitters, emphatically wrapping the game up by slotting past goalie Pope in the 86th minute, capping off yet another vibrant personal display.

In the Ribs of Beef after the game, it was a pleasure for the delectable Denise and me to meet up with Agent Watts (at his first match since the pandemic started), his partner

Claire and their young son Jack who'd momentously been attending his first-ever Norwich City game. They, too, reside just up the road from me in Chesterfield. Basking in the glow of the 2-0 triumph, it was heart-warming to observe Jack taking the match day experience in his stride, proudly wearing his City shirt that sported his name on the back, satisfied that his favourite player Kenny McLean had played a stormer. Crucially, he now had his feet firmly on that soon-to-be familiar, well-trodden path to Norwich, Norfolk and also elsewhere in the footballing pyramid; but principally, the A17, the A47, tractors, caravans, East Midlands Railways, victories, defeats, championships and relegations...

Joined by Sheffield-based Richard, we all blissfully made our way over Fye Bridge for the short stroll to our 'curry house of dreams', commonly known as Ali Tandoori, for a victory meal. I told you it was going to be a good weekend.

CHAPTER 17
NEWCASTLE UNITED (H)
10TH APRIL 2022

M uch has been made of Norwich's self-funded operating model and the apparent limitations to progression that this places on the team. But regarding the thorny issue of club ownership, you really ought to be careful about what you wish for. After all, the Football League is awash with floundering outfits that have been seriously mismanaged in the boardroom in recent times; Derby County, Birmingham City, Portsmouth and, of course, Ipswich Town immediately springing to mind.

Last weekend's opponents, Burnley FC, were acquired back in December 2020 by US management firm ALK Capital. Classed as a 'leveraged buyout', this type of deal has become an intrinsic part of football in recent times, with arguably the most high-profile being the purchase of Manchester United by the Glazer family. It is fair to say that plenty of risk is involved. Burnley, a club that was debt-free with cash reserves under the previous ownership, looks a very different operation these days. And just five days after their 2-0 defeat to the Canaries, they sacked Sean Dyche after a mammoth ten-year stint at the helm of the Lancashire club. With eight games left, only time will tell whether this was a huge gamble by ALK Capital smacking of blind panic or a roll of the dice that paid off spectacularly. Could it possibly be that the club's financial situation is so heavily intertwined with Premier League survival that it forced them to pull the trigger? On another note, those with an 'eagle eye' will also have spotted that Norwich's last three league victories have each resulted in the defeated opposition's manager getting the boot (after Rafa Benitez and Claudio Ranieri).

Before Norwich's next match, at Old Trafford against the Red Devils of Manchester, we were reminded of their supporters' unrest at ownership. Casey Brown of the Manchester Evening News reported that fan group 'The 1958' were planning a protest against the Glazer family before and during the game calling for the 'head of the snake' to be removed. The march was due to commence at 2pm before reaching the ground an hour later. Fans would then stay outside for a further seventeen minutes, symbolising the seventeen years that the Glazers have been in charge of the club.

By the time the Manchester latecomers gained access to the stadium, their team were already a goal to the good, Elanga dispossessing a dithering Ben Gibson before playing in Ronaldo for his first goal of the afternoon. At the half-hour mark, they appeared to have assumed total control, with the Portuguese international notching his second by way of a free header...dare I mention, from a corner. At this point, the majority of the whopping crowd of 73,381 smugly lolled back in their seats, safe in the knowledge that three points were securely in the bank, especially when considering the general lack of successful fightbacks that Norwich have produced throughout the season.

However, Red Devil panic stations were activated on the stroke of halftime when Kieran Dowell pulled a goal back with a close-range free header of his own. Norwich then took over, looking the better side. Magically, seven minutes after the resumption of the second half, Pukki tied the game up by interestingly slotting past David de Gea via the near post rather than his trademark finish of going across the goalkeeper. It was always the Canaries who looked like they were going to go on and snatch a match-winning third, with Milot Rashica having a fine effort saved by the keeper's outstretched hand while Sam Byram also saw a far-post header clear the bar. The conceited Old Trafford faithful were now uneasy in those smug seats of theirs...

It was left to Ronaldo to bail his team out by scoring his third of the afternoon (his second hat-trick in his last three league games) from a free-kick that Krul got a good hand to but ultimately failed to keep out of his net. Final score: Manchester United 3 Norwich City 2.

During the afternoon, you could sense that things were not going right for Manchester United, both off and on the pitch. There were genuine signs of unrest. And yet, as the afternoon's other results began to filter through, the league table showed that they could quite easily finish in the top 4 and claim a Champions League berth.

If the jury was still out for the Burnley fans who were still making their minds up about the ownership of ALK Capital and the Manchester United faithful so unhappy with the Glazer family that they had taken to the streets in protest, then it's correct to report that the Toon Army of Newcastle United (City's next opponents) are absolutely, deliriously happy with the recent takeover of the Tyneside club by Saudi Arabia's Public Investment Fund (PIF). They're not interested one iota in the kingdom's much-publicised and criticised human rights issues (with no apparent appetite to transform) and that the wealth is compromised; all they're concerned with is that they are now (possibly) the richest club in the world.

As I sauntered along Wherry Road on the way down to the stadium, enjoying the afternoon sun while trying to mind my own business, I was joined by a chap who said his name was Andrew. A Newcastle fan, he may have partaken in a few pre-match beers (not a crime on a matchday, as I well know). Also, there was maybe a chance that other substances could have been in play as he certainly appeared over-energetic as he surprisingly asked me, "Are you a Norwich fan?" I must admit that this was very perceptive of him as he had ingeniously spotted that I was modelling the 2015/2016 half and half yellow and green home shirt plus a bar scarf of the same colours. He then enquired, "What do you think of the takeover at the Toon then?"

My reply was tentative and low-key. After all, I think we can all appreciate that approaching a football stadium ten minutes before kick-off is not the perfect place or opportunity to have a deep and meaningful conversation about the myriad of trials and tribulations that come with a topic as complex as a change of football club ownership. In other words, there is nothing to be gained. "Not sure, to be honest. I've not looked into it too deeply, although, of course, I am aware that you've picked up form and a lot of points after the £90 million splurge on new players in January." As he nodded to my answer, I then thought it would be better to deflect the spotlight by asking him a question. "What do you think about the fact that Newcastle appears to be getting plenty of stick from opposition fans and journalists over the takeover in comparison to clubs who have undertaken similar deals, such as Manchester City?"

I could sense Andrew instantly warming to the challenge of answering my query. Aided by Dutch courage, he'd probably instigated many similar conversations with random strangers in recent months. "Yes, no, look", he impressively started off, in the manner of any one of a number of Premier League head coaches in a pre-match interview, before returning to basics. "I fucking love the fact that my club is now fucking loaded, wouldn't any fan? It is now our chance to shine, and everybody else can go fuck themselves. Why aye, man!" As he skipped off towards the South Stand, no doubt looking for his next examinee, I swear I could hear him whistle a 'Blaydon Races/Fog on the Tyne' medley…

During the weekend, Norwich City FC were celebrating 50 years since they had momentously first gained entry to the top-flight of domestic football. On Monday, April 24th 1972, a 2-1 win against Orient (with goals from Kenny Foggo and Graham Paddon) had sealed promotion with a 1-1 draw at Watford a few days later, securing the Division

Two title. The team, built by gritty, no-nonsense manager Ron Saunders was famed for its fitness, strength and character. The current vintage would need to display all these characteristics to mimic the win half a century ago.

Newcastle United hadn't won any of their opening 14 games of the season and had only managed to secure one victory out of the first 20. At that stage, they were in serious danger, with many people tipping them for a drop into the Championship. However, since their January transfer window binge, they had won nine of thirteen games played and were comfortably mid-table. There was no doubt that interesting times lay ahead for the St. James Park outfit, particularly concerning the inherited wealth, the calibre of player that this can attract and the trophies that can be subsequently acquired. And not for the first time this season, the afternoon's fixture would be contested by two clubs with polar opposite financial models.

Kieran Dowell had two excellent opportunities to put Norwich ahead early on. Firstly he was put through on goal by a probing, bouncing pass from Normann but could only manage to clear the goalkeeper and the bar with a right-footed lob. He was then found in a similar position by a cut back from Pukki but again put his shot into the crowd. Who knows what could have happened if either (or both) of those attempts had gone in. What we do know is that when Norwich are in the ascendancy, such as against Burnley, they do manage to find a bit extra, just that 5% effort and endeavour that can make all the difference.

As it was, Newcastle's serially un-prolific Joelinton took centre stage to double his season's goal tally to four by putting his team into a halftime lead of 2-0, and with that, the game was over as a contest. At the start of the second period, Krul literally passed straight to Guimaraes, lurking on the edge of the area, who promptly dinked the ball back over the goalkeeper's head for a third much to the delight of the travelling fans.

After then watching Christoph Zimmermann, Sam Byram and Mathias Normann needlessly and aimlessly giving the ball away, I observed the strange spectacle of Pierre Lees-Melou spectacularly falling to the floor, clutching his head after being hit by an innocuous-looking stray pass. Let's be clear here, he was playing football on a football pitch and not playing the slot machines at California Cliffs. He should not have been flabbergasted that a travelling football was in his vicinity. Expectedly there was no concern or alarm from absolutely anyone as, after a very short while indeed, a teammate casually walked past and lifted him up to his feet. At this precise moment, I asked myself a question "Neil, do you want to carry on watching this bunkum for the next half an hour, or would you prefer an early arrival in The Ribs of Beef?"

The Ribs of Beef has been owned by Roger and Anthea Cawdron for nearly forty years now. Enjoying one of the most picturesque locations in the City, it's perched on the edge of the River Wensum on the opposite side of the road to the much-photographed and painted Quayside area. This friendly 'local' has a reputation for having a strong and loyal following with a mission of ensuring 'customers return not as strangers but as friends'. As we are all well aware by now, history is never far from the flinty surface in Norwich, and there is no difference here with the 'Ribs' first being registered as an ale house in 1743. In 1929, the then owners Youngs, Crawshay and Youngs decided on a name change to the Fye Bridge Tavern (with the bridge being adjacent to the pub). Fast forward to 1958, and new owners Bullards took over the hostelry and then promptly de-licensed it. And that was that.

For the next 27 years, the building played host to, amongst other things, an antique shop, an electrical outlet and also a lady's fashion boutique. It really is mind-boggling to think of this particular part of Norwich without the well-established and comforting site of The Ribs of Beef being here; such is the high regard for this much-loved institution. Thankfully, in 1985 Roger and Anthea purchased the building and swiftly re-licensed it back as The Ribs of Beef.

The amiable and vastly travelled Jon Power has been the manager for the last six years. Arriving in the Fine City fourteen years ago to be closer to his Norfolk-based parents, he'd experienced the licensed trade when running a pool bar in London and then followed this up at the Mad Moose in the heart of Norwich's Golden Triangle area. Since being in the 'Ribs', he admits that real ale has become 'his thing' and enjoys visiting suchlike establishments in NR3, in particular the Leopard, the Artichoke and the Plasterers Arms. He always aims to have a constantly changing selection of interesting East Anglian guest ales available, plus recognised house staples such as Woodforde's Wherry, Wolf Golden Jackal and Adnams Ghost Ship.

I always think Jon runs a tight, very efficient ship. On arrival, you will obtain an immediate friendly greeting (from himself and/or one of his staff) who will direct you to an available seat and then take your order. Anyone who is not welcome will be diligently met at the door and effectively not allowed access ensuring appreciative customers enjoy their time spent in a safe and comfortable environment.

Like many other landlords and pub managers who I've spoken to since August, Jon sees his long-term future in his pub and, just like Stephen George at the Kings Head, has no intention of making any big changes any time soon; there's nothing broken so keep it as it is.

I was initially met in the 'Ribs' by the delectable Denise, who was rather pleased with herself after a successful afternoon of retail therapy. Her happiness and enthusiasm certainly rubbed off very quickly on me. It was either that or the tasty Nene Valley Big Bang Theory beer I was drinking, a 5.3% wonderfully balanced west coast pale ale. In fact, by the time Sheffield-based Richard had joined us, I had just about banished City's defeat into that rubbish bin at the back of my mind that is especially reserved for shite Norwich performances.

However, I thought it was still worth momentarily re-visiting the over-the-top reactions of the visiting supporters that we had witnessed within Carrow Road a short while earlier. Enjoy your goals, your victory and your day by all means, but the one thing that could be of benefit to the Toon Army in future would be a sense of perspective. It has become nauseatingly common for fans of many clubs, especially the bigger and richer ones, to view the fortunes of their side as the definitive barometer of their own lives. With this in mind, it was still peculiar to see a celebratory Newcastle supporter (don't worry, I've checked, and it definitely wasn't Andrew) grotesquely waving a wad of ten pounds notes in the air in an attempt at taunting the unimpressed Norwich faithful. It was as though he really felt that his club's newfound riches were intertwined with his own. His team will have far bigger and wealthier fish to fry next season, of course, than this current punch-drunk Canary outfit.

CHAPTER 18
WEST HAM UNITED (H)
10TH APRIL 2022

For City's next game, away at Aston Villa, Tim Krul implored his teammates to get a win for their boss Dean Smith. From past experiences when there have been similar pleas, it has never, ever gone well. "Let's do it for the fans, let's do it for the manager, let's do it for (insert player's name here)" always ends in defeat. Would there be a similar conclusion against Villa?

In the days leading up to the match, Aston Villa fan group 'Project B6' announced that they would be unfurling a banner, paid for by fans, paying homage to Smith. One of their own, he is fondly remembered for his role at the club, where he led them to promotion into the Premier League and then kept their heads above water for the next two seasons. I think we can all agree it was a touching gesture by a band of supporters who were eager to show their respect and love for him.

There will be a few individuals on planet earth who are totally oblivious to the fact that Smith has been a supporter of The Villans since boyhood and was their manager for three years before they fired him towards the end of 2021 after a five-game losing run. The people who are not aware will be the types who take off for months on end on a solo trek into the outback of Australia or to row the Atlantic single-handed. Literally, everyone else will know.

Why's that Neil, I hear you ask. Well, I'll tell you why. Every single opportunity that Deano gets in a press conference to mention Aston Villa, he gleefully takes.

"AstonVillaaremyclubVillaVillaAstonVillaIsignedhimfor-AstonVillaAstonAstonVillaWelookedathimwhenIwasat-VillaVillaAstonFamilyareVillafansAstonAstonVilla-IbroughtthimthroughatVillaAstonAstonVillaEnjoyed-mythreeyearsatAstonVillaVillaAstonAstonItwasanhonour-tobemanagerofAstonVillaVillaVillaI'vealreadywon-therethisseasonwithAstonVillaAstonVillaAstonIt'salways-beenatoughgamewhenI'vebeentherewithVillaVillaAston-VillaEveryoneknowsI'maVillafanVillaVillaAstonVilla."

Now I can't say that I've got anything specific against the team from Birmingham, like I've got nothing against Reading, Cheltenham, Carlisle or Wealdstone, for that matter. It's just that, for me, there's nowt special about them either (I appreciate that this is a sentiment that will no doubt be reciprocated by Villa fans about Norwich too). What I do know is that (and you have to say the next bit in a Kevin Keegan accent) "I'd love it, love it" for him to stop incessantly harping on about them and concentrate solely on what he has done and what he will do for the team who are called Norwich City.

Tim Krul's appeal to his teammates fell on deaf ears, with the Canaries expectedly limping to a 0-2 loss, the nineteenth time they had failed to score this season. It also signalled an end to the interminable run of 'must-win games' that, on reflection, started as far back as September when Watford were the visitors to Carrow Road. With rejuvenated Burnley snatching a late victory (at Watford) this meant that the inevitable demotion was finally rubber-stamped with four games still to go. In truth, it had been 'death by a thousand cuts', a record sixth relegation from the Premier League and crucially a demoralising second in the last three campaigns. Repercussions swiftly commenced amongst many supporters who wanted to "Sack the board/Sack (Sporting Director) Stuart Webber/Sack Delia and Michael." There was also a random clamour for a nation-state to come to the rescue...or an oligarch...or maybe even a US management firm. There didn't appear to be many people who were inclined to speak out against Dean Smith at this stage, even though he had overseen a relegation featuring two losing streaks each of six league games (plus, it was feasible that he could quite easily finish the season off with getting beaten in the last seven matches); the goodwill shown towards him solely being linked to the fact that he had yet to sign a player for the club. Ultimately he'd failed in his mission to keep Norwich in the Premier League.

If he is to remain at the club for next season's tilt at the Championship, he'd be wise not to keep monotonously mentioning the club he supports. After all, Daniel Farke's team romped to the title in 2018-2019, a mammoth 18 points in front of Smith's Aston Villa outfit, who finished the regular season in fifth position before hobbling to promotion via the play-offs.

Right, let's get back to ownership issues. During the week leading up to City's penultimate home game against West Ham United, Simon Stone of the BBC reported that Burnley would need to pay back a 'significant proportion' of a £65 million loan at the end of the season if relegated. The loan had been surprisingly taken out during the club's takeover by ALK Capital in December 2020. The Clarets say that in the event of relegation, it is 'satisfied' that it would retain the support of its lenders. On the £65 million loan specifically, it is outlined within Burnley's accounts that an annual interest rate of 8% is payable, and only these interest payments are due (IF they remain in the Premier League) until December 2025, when the whole amount will have to be paid. For some (unexplained) reason, relegation brings the end repayment date forward significantly, hence the throw of the dice a few weeks ago that resulted in Sean Dyche getting the boot.

On the face of it, the loan malarkey looks a right dog's dinner and no doubt a tad scary for Burnley supporters. For a club that were famed for being debt-free with cash reserves prior to the takeover, it's beyond belief that at that particular time, they needed to take out another £65 million, isn't it? After all, it appears that the buyout was made by somehow using the club's own money, PLUS the loan that they are now being charged 8% interest on. Bonkers, if you ask me. Like I've said before, you really have to be careful what you wish for with club ownership. Meanwhile, in other news, there were rumours surfacing of a planned pre-match protest before the Hammers game by some fans unhappy with the Norwich ownership...

It was dour and proud Yorkshireman Wiggy's last ever visit to the Fine City; the end of what had been a bloody good era. Accompanied by the delectable Denise and life and soul Paul, we were sat around a table in his favourite city centre pub (you know, the one with two names) as he explained, "It's not cos we're shite at the moment; it's just that I'm not well enough to keep making the journey." Now based in Clungunford, Shropshire, it was a four-hour cross-country drive that he had been more than willing to regularly make until quite recently, but now he had succumbed to debilitating health issues. His season ticket had duly been cancelled, and he wasn't even staying over into tomorrow afternoon to watch the West Ham match – he had just travelled to have a few pints, a farewell meal in the Ali Tandoori, and then say his goodbyes. We had a good laugh about his unhealthy and yet genuine contempt for a team from his home county, who he was always eager to refer to as' the White Shite' (due to the colour of their kit). We reminisced about pre-season away trips to Raith Rovers and Glasgow Celtic, top-notch drinking sessions in places like Preston, Wigan and Derby and revelled in recalling the many joyous promotions we'd witnessed together over the years (Holty, Cameron Jerome and Pukki). "Just for today though, let's not go there with the shite seasons", he appealed, and we didn't.

Nestled away just up Timberhill (one of the oldest recorded city streets), the official title of the pub is the Gardeners Arms, and yet if you were on your way up Gentleman's Walk asking for directions to it, there's a fair chance even the locals would not know where you were talking about. However, if you were to enquire as to the whereabouts of the Murderers, they would duly oblige and show you the way (and let's face it, the sobriquet sounds far more alluring and thrilling, doesn't it?). One of the last family-owned pubs in the centre of Norwich, it's full of wooden beams, steps taking you up or down to nooks and crannies and dates back to 1530.

But where's 'The Murderers' name come from Neil, I hear you ask. Well, thanks for inquiring. Back in 1895, the pub was being run by husband and wife team Henry and Maria Wilby, but on the 5th of January of that year, Henry suffered a heart attack and died on the premises. A daughter named Mildred (also known as Millie), who had recently separated from her husband Frank Miles, moved into the Gardeners to help her mother run the business in what must have been a very difficult period after her husband's death. The estranged Frank was working for local brewery Morgans and was living above the Crown & Anchor on Calvert Street in the City, just off Colegate. He desperately wanted to be reconciled with Millie but suspected that she might have been seeing another man. And one night, in a pre-meditated attack, he went into the pub and bludgeoned her with a 'bung picker' that he had taken earlier from the brewery. She died just three days later, meaning poor old Maria had lost both a husband and a daughter within the space of a few months.

West Ham United arrived at Carrow Road fresh from a traumatic 0-1 defeat at Eintracht Frankfurt in the Europa League Semi-Final 2nd leg, a game where everything had gone wrong for them (on aggregate, they had lost the tie 1-

3). They had played over seventy minutes with ten men after Aaron Creswell had been dismissed in the 19th minute. His boss, David Moyes, had also seen red and been sent to the stands in what had been a heated evening in Germany. The game would have taken a lot out of the Hammers both physically and emotionally, and they could be seen by Dean Smith's team as being ripe for putting on a good show against, regaining some pride and respect in the process. Now that their fate had been decided and the relegation shackles had been unlocked, it was deemed a free hit for City, a great opportunity to get three points and put some smiles back on the faces of their beleaguered fan base. Nevertheless, West Ham were known for their general strength and physicality, whereas Norwich simply weren't. They were also rather good at defending and attacking set pieces and Norwich (well, you can complete the sentence if you wish).

I'm pleased to report that in his pre-match press conference Dean Smith somehow managed to squeeze in yet another obligatory reference to his former club when asked about his thoughts on the East London team. He said, "When I was at Aston Villa two years ago, we were fighting with them to avoid relegation." All was well with the world…

There was no 'Hammer Hangover' as Norwich were thrashed 0-4. It didn't take a magical performance from the visitors; they just did their jobs, setting the scene in the opening half an hour as they went two up after a couple of big old errors from City stopper Tim Krul. As all the best music hall 'comedians' would have said, "If the goalie had put his head in his hands, he would have surely dropped that too! I thank you!" I'd like to envisage current second-choice custodian Angus Gunn banging on Smith's door first thing on Monday morning, demanding to know why's he's not been given a chance in front of the failing Dutchman, who's had a poor time of it lately. The initial response would likely start off with "Yes, no, look. Well Angus, when I was manager at Aston Villa, we had a goalkeeper who blah blah blah blah blah."

Lamentably, throughout the ninety minutes, Norwich couldn't muster the pride in performance that we had all hoped for. They were heading into the Championship with not so much as a whimper. As a comparison, on the same afternoon, perennial underdogs Wycombe Wanderers had been winning a League One Play-Off Semi-Final tie against highly-rated MK Dons and had (against the odds) got through to the final. Their boss is Gareth Ainsworth, charismatic and every bit a rock star. After the game, he proudly told BBC Three Counties Radio that his players were heroes and that they'd been sensational. They'd effectively operated a deep press, chucked their bodies on the line, blocked things and headed things. Theirs was a defensive set-up that he was delighted with. Everyone was happy to run around.

Norwich City, once again, had been the polar opposite...

A short stroll around the corner from our customary Norwich base on Duke Street lies the Playhouse Bar. Situated alongside St George's Bridge, it's an ideal place to recuperate after witnessing a totally abject yellow and green performance at Carrow Road, and I was soon into my stride after meeting back up with the 'delectable' one. If you want to see a giant HP sauce bottle on wheels, skulls and masks and a Lego display under a glass-topped bar, then this is the place for you too. There are three real ales and a cacophony of hot beverages and herbal teas. There's Erykah Badu, TLC and Kelis (singing 'sugar honey iced tea' – I see what they did there) quietly and unobtrusively piped through the speakers for the pleasure of the eclectic mix of friendly clientele. There's a well-maintained outside seating area where the 'House Rules' include "No top, no pop. No shoes, no booze. No circus skills. No acoustic guitar!!!" Thoughtfully they even have hot water bottles and blankets for hire for when it gets a tad chilly. There's no one shouting and bawling, just a well-behaved crowd enjoying the laid-back vibe. Oh, and there's a fish tank. There's an upside-down sky scene on the bar ceiling with more skyscrapers than you can shake a Ferris wheel, a hot air balloon or a polo mint at (if you know, you know). You could quite easily be in a bar in Copenhagen or Malmo with everybody minding their own business in that rather pleasant and refreshing type of Scandinavian way. They're doing crosswords, playing chess or having a good old natter. The delectable Denise loves it here and, as dour and proud Yorkshireman Wiggy would probably say, "You can come here at any time, not just when Norwich have been shite!"

CHAPTER 19

TOTTENHAM HOTSPUR (H)

22ND MAY 2022

Since returning from his long-term injury issues, defender, Sam Byram, had meteorically soared up the Canary pecking order in the last couple of months, with his head coach admitting that he had him in mind as a future club captain. Remarkably he had recently replaced stalwarts Max Aarons and then Ben Gibson in the starting eleven. He was also the latest player to go to the press (in this case to The Pink Un's Connor Southwell), a la Tim Krul, as he explained, "We need to show personal pride and pride for the fans and give them something to be excited about ahead of next season. As a team, we need to show what we're going to be about by showing a bit of fight and hunger."

Then, just prior to the re-arranged midweek fixture away at Leicester, youngster Jon Rowe entered the fray from a slightly left-of-field position. Yet to make a first-team start, but speaking on behalf of his more experienced teammates, he told the club's official channel, "I think it is unacceptable that we have got to this point, but all we can

. do is focus on the future and look forward to what we can control. What is done is done; that is the past. We have got to make ourselves better for whatever we face, and we come up against Leicester on Wednesday and the team will be looking to change our ways. I just think it is all about our pride and decorum. We need to let the fans know that we are still fighting for this club and to keep our dignity about us."

I think we all know where this is heading...

Jamie Vardy netted twice as the Foxes effortlessly moved through the gears with Norwich old boy, fan favourite and acknowledged club saviour James Maddison getting a third, condemning his previous employers to a fifth straight loss. They had now conceded a mammoth 78 goals in 36 games while failing to hit the net themselves in 21 of them.

There was a peculiar and admittedly tenuous hope on the horizon that points could be gained at Molineux on Sunday. Opponents Wolverhampton Wanderers were just one of an elite number of a small but perfectly formed group of three teams who had not managed to defeat or even score against Norwich City this season in two games played. Where it had appeared to be a rather easy task for most sides to locate the soft Canaries underbelly Burnley (with a 0-0 draw and a 0-2 defeat), Brighton (two 0-0 shutouts), and Wolves (0-0 at Carrow Road and a 0-1 FA Cup loss) had astonishingly and incomprehensibly struggled. I acknowledge Burnley had also endured a poor campaign and continued to dally with relegation but Brighton, still on course for their best-ever top-flight finishing position and Wolves, still challenging for a Europa Conference League place, were two fine footballing teams. I know, I know I'm clutching at some incredibly brittle straws here, but still…Football certainly is a strange game, isn't it? And, due to the above sequence of results having already occurred, it wouldn't be too much of a surprise if Norwich remained undefeated against the Wolves after yet another 90 minutes.

There was an end-of-season feel in the air as referee Tony Harrington got the game underway in the West Midlands. It was definitely a subdued atmosphere from the home fans, unusually reticent in cranking up the volume to the normal levels experienced at Molineux. In fact, some felt a need to 'boo' their team off at the break, after Pukki had given the visitors a deserved lead, wrong-footing goalkeeper and another City old boy John Ruddy in the process. There were no 'You're not fit to wear the shirt' banners on display though, which have been a feature at this ground a few times on past visits.

Wolves equalised ten minutes into the second half, finally managing to find the net against Norwich after a combined total of 235 minutes, nearly four hours of football. Neither side were able to find a winner as the game petered out into a 1-1 draw, a result that Dean Smith said had "stopped the bleeding" after the latest run of losses. It was obvious that during the next few weeks, there was to be a whole lot of soul searching, hand wringing, mudslinging and demands for reasons for what had gone wrong for much of this wretched season. But before all that, there was just the one league game to fulfil: at home to the Spurs from Tottenham.

Tottenham Hotspur is a great name, don't you think? A unique, exciting and distinguishing suffix in a football world full of Towns, Uniteds and, of course, Citys. But how did they acquire that name Neil, I hear you ask. Well, believe it or not, the story started way back in the late fourteenth, early fifteenth century with a somewhat flamboyant chappie called Sir Henry Percy, an English knight and son of the Earl of Northumberland. Renowned as a ferocious and courageous fighter in battle, the name 'Hotspur' was bestowed upon him by one of his sworn enemies, the Scottish army, due to his speed and eagerness to advance in battle, not to mention the effective, expert use of his riding spurs. His overall nickname thus became 'Harry Hotspur'.

After playing a key part in an English victory at the Battle of Homildon Hill in 1402, the Percy family was awarded the Borough of Tottenham by the King, commencing the link of Northumberland's finest with this part of North London.

Fast forward over four hundred years, and a group of sports-mad boys were to form a cricket club in the area, naming it 'Hotspur Cricket Club' in deference to Harry's battling exploits. Keen to continue their exertions into the winter months, the cricketers then increased their sporting portfolio with the creation of a football club, finally settling on the elongated name of Tottenham Hotspur Football Club in order to avoid any obvious confusion with the summer outfit.

Now, this has got me thinking. Just imagine, if the Fine City had momentously been paid a visit by or bestowed an honour on one of the knights from 'back in the day', what our beloved football team could now be named. A quick scan through a list of well-known, swashbuckling cavaliers reveals that many were awarded illustrious nicknames, for example:

- **Robert Guiscard** – 'The Crafty' as he was 'as wily as a fox'
- **Rodrigo Diaz de Vivar** – 'El Cid', sounding remarkably like a latter-day Costa's villain
- **Sir William Marshal** – 'The Glutton' which admittedly you'd hope was due to him having a voracious appetite for food but is more likely to be related to his general lust for battle
- ....and my favourite, **Richard I** – 'The Lionhearted'

Therefore, considering the recent heartfelt, public appeals from Tim Krul, Sam Byram and Jon Rowe for pride, hunger, dignity and fight I think it would be a cracking idea that as it's the end of the season, for one game only, we should be temporarily renamed Norwich Lionhearts! "COOOMMME ON YOUUUU LIONHEEEEAAAARTS."

So, on Sunday at a smidgeon after five to four, with Fleetwood Mac's 'The Chain' reverberating around 'The Carra', I'll be watching with interest as the players take to the field. Wouldn't it be great if 'Dan the Tannoy Man' announced: "Ladies and Gentlemen, Boys and Girls, welcome your teams to Carrow Road – NORWICH LIONHEARTS VERSUS TOTTENHAM HOTSPUR!!!"

The delectable one and my good self arrived in Norwich in the early afternoon on the Friday before the game and immediately headed to the Fat Cat on West End Street. It seemed apt that we should go there before the last game of the season as we were also there way, way back in August before the opening league fixture against Liverpool. On that day, we'd witnessed CAMRA presenting owner Colin Keatley with one of their 50 Gold Awards, a richly deserved honour for this back street boozer where you're always guaranteed 'a good pint'.

So what makes 'the Cat' so special? It's a place that visitors from near and far have enthusiastically been seeking out for over thirty years. Well, believe it or not, Colin believes he's been the beneficiary of a huge slice of luck, being in the right place at the right time. Back in 1991, when he bought the pub (it was then a run-down place known as the New Inn), he explained that there were only around half a dozen decent real ale establishments in Norwich. He 'did it up' a bit, 'put on some decent beers' and attracted a healthy trade straight away, 'hitting the ground running' with his initial view being that (providing everything was still going well) he'd probably stay at the helm for around ten years before selling up and moving on to a new project.

It's an understatement to emphasise that he's most obviously selling himself short when he puts his success down mainly to good fortune. Let me try and explain...

For starters, early in the morning, you can stroll along Adelaide Street (where you'll find the pub's side entrance), and there'll be one of his employees hosing down the pavement making sure everything's clean for neighbours who'll be walking past during the day. There are no empty glasses, cigarette butts or crisp packets remaining within the outside seating areas from the night before. They've been collected and responsibly disposed of with the tables and chairs respectively placed back in position, ready for when the punters start to arrive in a couple of hours time. Meanwhile, behind the scenes inside the premises, lines are diligently being cleaned for the draught beers while a host of ales and traditional ciders are waiting to be dispensed from the expertly maintained tap room. The interior of the pub is spick and span, with the tables clean and Fat Cat branded beer mats strategically placed on them. Toilets are scrubbed down (and will be regularly cleaned throughout the day). This is not luck; this is a combination of effective organisation and hard graft.

Once the doors open for business, there are over 20 real ales plus around ten traditional ciders for thirsty customers to choose from, plus a substantive offering of other drinks. There are the usual snack offerings commonly found in other pubs, but here you'll also find a battery of pork pies tactically placed in a glass-fronted fridge, directly behind the main part of the bar, in full view and seriously tempting anyone who's a tad peckish. If breweriana is your thing, then the walls are bedecked with old pub signs, antique brewery and beer adverts, a wealth of pictures, paintings and photos, plus an impressive collection of vintage whisky water jugs. Wherever you choose to sit, there is always something of interest to look at. Again, all this is not down to luck; this is down to an owner who appreciates what products customers want to purchase and acknowledges that they prefer a comfortable interior that makes them feel at home in a place that anyone could call their 'local'.

Colin is a self-professed 'old style landlord', and it is here where he particularly flourishes. He's keen to walk around collecting the empty glasses; he has a brief chat with absolutely everyone, as he works his way around, making sure that they're comfortable, making sure that they feel welcome, making sure that they feel valued. He then gets a pint for himself before sitting down with customers for a more in-depth confab, finding out what's what, finding out the latest news from the streets of Norwich. He's effortlessly working the room, naturally networking without having attended the expensive courses that corporate big wigs have attended in order to be instructed on how to do this.

And he's 'done alright' for himself over the years. The success of the Fat Cat (and the White Lion on Oak Street before it) has enabled him to purchase other freeholds in the City, such as The Wherry on Lawson Road (now the Brewery Tap), the Mustard Pot on Thorpe Road (now the Fat Cat & Canary) and The Perseverance on Adelaide Street (initially renamed the Fat Percy but now Harry's Soul Station). He understands that he's now operating 'in a different world', particularly with the purchase of free houses that are far more expensive than they once were. It's also almost unheard of these days for a pub to be successful without doing food or cocktails, for that matter.

After over fifty years spent in the licensing trade, Colin has no intention of calling it a day yet, as he's still obviously enjoying himself at the Fat Cat as it continues to thrive. There's further good news as well regarding the future for this bastion of real ale as when he does decide to call it a day, son Will (who has been involved at 'the Cat' himself for the last fourteen years) will take over the reins. For those of us who love to see stability at our favourite pubs, we can all breathe a sigh of relief and continue to look forward to paying a visit to this wonderful establishment …

There was definitely 'something strange in the air' early on Sunday morning in the Fine City, and I'm not just talking about what the Spurs fans were smoking. I'm sure I'm no different to most people in the fact that I can be sitting reading a newspaper, minding my own business, when a couple of people will come and sit nearby and then proceed to talk as though I am invisible. Bear in mind, I'm six foot tall, weigh (ahem) upwards of fifteen stones and on this particular day wearing a vivid yellow and green Norwich shirt. Picture the scene, if you please; I'm sitting alone in the centre of the Glasshouse beer garden with the sun shining down on me with the unique and beautiful cathedral chimes kindly advising me of every fifteen minutes that I've been here. I've just polished off a light breakfast of scrambled egg on toast and am preparing to do the sudoku in the previous day's Norwich Evening News, a choice of white coffee and iced water to the right of the table. The door opens and, at first glance, an inoffensive and yet admittedly well-dressed (for this time of day) middle-aged couple comes outside, deciding to sit at a shaded rather than sunny table after a short chat. They're quite giggly and touchy-feely, and it is soon rather obvious that they've not known each other for too long; he's describing his morning commute into London before briefly explaining what he does for a living. They politely discuss whether to 'go to the coast or not' in that non-committed way of a new couple, careful not to offend each other before he casually asks her, "So what can you tell me about yourself then?"

Her answer: "Well, apparently I'm very good at blow

jobs, Gary", to which he immediately endorses with "Yep, I can certainly vouch for that!" There are then more playful giggles from the pair before she gushes, "Oh stop it", whilst giving good old Gary a playful slap on his shoulder ", You're making me blush."

And there's more…

A few hours later, I'm sitting outside the front of the Playhouse Bar, now accompanied by the delectable Denise, and tell her about the conversation I overheard earlier at the Glasshouse. As usual, there are plenty of people going about their business here on St Georges Street; it really is a busy walking, cycling, scootering thoroughfare between St Andrews Street and Colegate. Another innocuous-looking couple tentatively approaches the bar entrance, shopping bags in hand, hesitating whether to go in or not. The woman suggests, "Well, why don't we go in here for a pit stop and have a nice cuppa" before adding, "We can then go home and watch some porn if ya want?" He shrugs his shoulders before confirming, "Yeah, that'll be alright, I guess", with all the enthusiasm of someone who's just been offered a ham sandwich with a packet of salt and vinegar crisps.

"Did I just hear that correctly Neil?" enquires a wide-eyed Denise. You most certainly did, my dear. You most certainly did.

And there's more…

Two young ladies, I'm guessing late teens/early twenties, come and sit at the table behind us. They're eager to find out what each other had been up to the previous evening. Girl #1 starts off proceedings. "So, come on, tell me, how did it go last night?"

Girl #2 answers, "Yeah pretty good, thanks. I decided to have a threesome with Liam and James. To be honest, I prefer Liam out of the two, so I did all the interesting bits with him and just let James do his bit at the back."

Denise slowly moved her head towards me and with an earnest look on her face, quietly enquired, "What the hell is going on around here today…do you think someone's slipped something into the water?"

On the walk down King Street to the ground, I couldn't help but notice how excitable and keyed up the Spurs fans were. They informed me that their team needed just a point from the afternoon's game to ensure a fourth-place finish in the Premier League, thereby cementing a spot in next season's Champions League. My initial thoughts were that their exuberant behaviour felt way over the top to be celebrating completing the season behind Manchester City (who were to finish a full 22 points in front of them), Liverpool and Chelsea. But then I thought back to the heady days of May 1993 when Andy Linighan headed past Chris Woods to win the FA Cup for Arsenal against Sheffield Wednesday, meaning that Norwich City's third-place finish in the inaugural Premier League had merited their entrance into the UEFA Cup, coming at a time when the Canaries were justifiably (although all-too-briefly) dining at the top table of football. The following day I remember being sat at Edgbaston watching a one-day cricket international between England and Australia, a contest memorable for Robin Smith clonking a glorious 167 not out. It also sticks in the memory banks on a personal level as I sat through the entire contest with a stupid grin on my face and a warm fuzzy feeling going around my body at the looping thought of watching my team on the European stage at last. With that recollection still fresh in mind, I sportingly (not like me, I can assure you) wished a few of the Tottenham fans 'all the best' whilst desperately hoping that Norwich could somehow, someway avoid defeat.

Can you remember the opening day match against Liverpool? Fresh off the back of the record-breaking, Championship-winning season, there was a full house singing proud choruses of 'On The Ball City' with the belief that we may just beat our illustrious opponents, albeit if we could catch them on an off day. Today, our much-loved anthem was being sung out of habit. There were no pre-match pyrotechnics and no vigorous waving of yellow and green flags. We were here because this is what we do. In truth, we were demoralised, we were beaten, we were battered and humiliated. Those Talksport protagonists had been right all along.

Match Report: You already know. It's the same report as it has been for most of the home defeats this season. Bright start > concede a sloppy, early goal > catastrophic error leads to a further concession > heads drop (players and fans) > opposition get the cigars out, taking the piss for the rest of the game, scoring goals when they want > referee blows whistle to end the game.

When Son Heung-Min had stroked the ball past Krul to make it 0-4 on the 70th minute, that had been enough for me. There to greet me at the 'emergency' early exit gate was a familiar face; a lady who'd been opening the gate for me to leave early on a regular basis since the Arsenal game in December. "See you later, duck" I said on my way out.

"Summer well, and I look forward to seeing you again at the end of July."

"See you later, my lovely", she replied with a lovely smile on her face. "Likewise, and you also have a great summer."

As I walked out of the concourse gloom into the warm sunlight of Carrow Road, an enormous tidal wave of relief surged over me. I would not have to make any more harrowing and excruciating visits here for another two months. It would be a time spent licking wounds, resting, recovering and building back strength, hope and expectation.

Because we've encountered many relegations and bad times before, haven't we? Granted, it's not easy, and yet we've always found a way to bounce back. We've been defeated in League Cup finals and FA Cup semi-finals and suffered other humbling cup losses against Bradford City, Bury, Port Vale, Crawley and (non-league) Luton. We've been traumatised after a 0-6 last day defeat at Fulham and humiliated by a 1-7 season-opening shocker against Colchester. Police horses have charged up Carrow Road to quell fan protests after the Brentford match in 1995, and we've absorbed the debilitating body blows of seeing Reeves, Sutton and the talismanic, totemic Buendia leave our beloved club all far, far too early.

But do you know what? We've had the thrill of seeing World Cup winner Martin Peters play in yellow and green and the overwhelming excitement of signing Darren Huckerby. I've been to Wembley in 2015 with my girls Paige and Alisha for the 2-0 victory over Middlesbrough – a day to treasure forever. We've witnessed the many promotions, all individually special and memorable. We've revelled in watching hat-tricks by MacDougall, Busby, Holt and Pukki, not to mention Justin's goal-of-the-season against Liverpool and Gossy's volley against Bayern Munich.

My 2022-2023 season ticket (with a new seat!) has already been purchased. The belief in my club and the hope in my heart is already returning.

I'm 'all in' for next season…are you?

ABOUT THE AUTHOR

It's only since being asked to form a few words for his wonderful book, that I realise I've been mates with Neil for well over 30 years. I wouldn't say we're especially close, but then we're blokes and we don't really do that kind of thing do we? A friendship formed in the workplace, developed in the dressing room but set firm at the bar. As I said – we're blokes, and that's usually how we roll.

Looking back, it's a friendship that on the face of it seems remarkably un-remarkable, but I think therein lies its beauty. We had similar interests and similar values, we worked hard - played hard, that kind of thing. Neil introduced me to some of life's more rewarding experiences – following the national team; a water-tight bat-pad forward defensive and humour-driven conversation to name but 3 (we'll pass on the Holsten Pils phase). As much as anything I guess what I really saw in Neil was affirmation of my own parent's principles and values that were applied to my upbringing.

We were close enough for me not even to consider it slightly odd that a kid from a working-class mining community in Chesterfield grows up an ardent Canary - it was Neil after all, and it would have seemed stranger had it been any other way. Accompanying him to Carrow Road for Tuesday night home fixtures in the early 90's seemed even more natural. Half a day off work, 6 hours in a car for a 90-minute game of football and as much "pub" time as you might be able to squeeze in. Sounds daft to a lot of people, but that's not really what it's all about. What it's really about is spending that time in the company of people that you truly value. It's about the conversation, the banter and discussions. The agreements and disagreements but never a hint of an argument or fall-out. The belly-bursting laughs and childish giggles. It's about climbing into bed in the small hours of a Wednesday morning feeling tired and dirty, dreading the alarm going off in 5 hours time, but already looking forward to doing it all over again.

What it's actually all about of course is knowing that you're a better person for the time you've spent in certain company – and that's Neil right there. Counting him as a friend will almost certainly bring a different perspective into your life, but one that will make you a better, more rounded individual for it. And having read this book you will hopefully have been given an insight to how good that might feel.

Chris Radford (5 June 2022)
Managing Director & Head Brewer,
Brampton Brewery Ltd
Supporter of *The Real Ale Canary*

ACKNOWLEDGEMENTS

Back in May 2021 when I commenced the exciting process of writing this, my first book, I didn't have a clue about how I, or the concept of the book for that matter, would be perceived or received. What I did know at that point was that I would need the assistance of a lot of people for help, advice, guidance, knowledge and contributions. But how would they react?

I'm more than pleased to report that I have been overwhelmed with the response to my requests and will be forever grateful for the unfailing backing of the many individuals who have directly contributed in their own specific way and also to the large group of family and friends (too many to mention here but you know who you are) who have provided me with continuous enthusiasm and support during this time.

And so, without further ado, I'd like to announce *The Real Ale Canary* 'Roll of Honour'. In no particular order:

Proofreader, Cheerleader and all-round Positivity Therapist - Paula Wigfield

Authors – Pauline Wilkie, Kevin Baldwin, Ed Couzens-Lake, Mick Dennis & Paddy Davitt

Pub Landlords, Managers & Brewery Owners – Craig McLaren, Simon Davey, Aey Allen, Elliot Dransfield, Dawn

Hopkins, Christian Hodgkinson, Stephen George, Mike Deal, Jon Power & Colin Keatley

Poet – Harry Exford

Cover Artist – Imogen Worthington

Contributors and Supporters – Billy Dearden, Rob Butler, Chris Radford (and all at Brampton Brewery)

Publisher – Robert Bannister of Bannister Publications

Newspapers – Eastern Daily Press and Norwich Evening News, for always being a valuable and trusty resource of all things yellow and green

Family – The delectable Denise, for always being available to listen and provide feedback, not only for this book but for life in general…

…and last but by no means least, my beautiful daughters Paige and Alisha for rubber-stamping the original idea and then driving me forward to completion.

"You can achieve anything you want to in this world… all you have to do is try."